1/24/02
steel is print
gas

The Underside
of
High-Tech

THE UNDERSIDE OF HIGH-TECH

TECHNOLOGY AND THE DEFORMATION OF HUMAN SENSIBILITIES _____

EDITED BY John W. Murphy,
Algis Mickunas, and
Joseph J. Pilotta

CONTRIBUTIONS IN SOCIOLOGY, NUMBER 59

GREENWOOD PRESS
NEW YORK • WESTPORT, CONNECTICUT • LONDON

Library of Congress Cataloging-in-Publication Data
Main entry under title:

The Underside of high-tech.

(Contributions in sociology, ISSN 0084–9278 ; no. 59)
Bibliography: p.
Includes index.
1. Technology and civilization—Addresses, essays,
lectures.   2. Technology—Social aspects—Addresses,
essays, lectures.   I. Murphy, John W.   II. Mickunas,
Algis.   III. Pilotta, Joseph J.   IV. Series.
HM221.U53   1986   303.4'83   85–27265
ISBN 0–313–24612–2 (lib. bdg. : alk. paper)

Library of Congress Catalog Card Number: 85–27265
ISBN: 0–313–24612–2
ISSN: 0084–9278

First published in 1986

Greenwood Press, Inc.
88 Post Road West, Westport, Connecticut 06881

Printed in the United States of America

The paper used in this book complies with the
Permanent Paper Standard issued by the National
Information Standards Organization (Z39.48–1984).

10 9 8 7 6 5 4 3 2 1

Contents

Introduction

John W. Murphy, Algis Mickunas, and Joseph J. Pilotta

The term "underside" used in the title of this collection of articles has two different yet interrelated meanings. First, it is intended to suggest that technology is far more than machinery. If the utilization of technology could be equated with the implementation of machines, then the histories of mechanization and technology would be identical. This, however, is not the case. Technology has a "worldview" that constitutes its underside and differentiates it from machinery. Most discussions of technology, nevertheless, overlook how this worldview can shape persons' perceptions of themselves, their environment, and society.

Second, the term "underside" refers to the undesirable consequences that can stem from the unmonitored growth of technology. Technology may have a seamy side that produces problems that are not logistical or the outcome of technical errors.[1] The image of the world may be altered irrevocably by the philosophy that subtends technology. Moreover, the writers in this collection contend that this worldview is instrumental in generating the illusion that technology is out of control, while fostering indifference about the human condition, otherwise known as alienation.

In this book, technology is treated as a philosophy. Although technology has concrete implications for social existence that require practical solutions for society to survive, logistical or technical remedies may not correct these problems. Instead, the philosophy of technology may have to be effectively challenged so that technology can be understood to be a tool that furthers humanly inspired aims.

Technology advances a style of rationality that subverts the spontaneity indigenous to human action. Because technological rationality, also known as instrumental reason, is disconnected from human desires, all measurements are believed to be standardized and precise.[2] This form of dualism elevates technological rationality to the paragon of reason. Accordingly, pristine measurements are assumed to supply order with legitimacy simply because of their objective and thus unprejudiced status. Technology, then, represents abstract rationality and not humanity, since the existential choices that accompany the use of technology are diminished. Technological rationality appears to be self-justifying, as it dominates social logic.[3]

Consequently, human existence is conceptualized technologically. The articles in this volume address five areas of social life that are most affected by this process. First, persons are supplied with a material identity, as the human body is compared to an objective thing. Because existential *pathos* is sequestered from the body, the human presence is transformed into a *korper*, or dead flesh.[4] The body is treated as a mechanism that causes behavior, thus transforming sensuality into an "instrumental structure."[5] This transmutation is revealed clearly in the papers by Esther Merves, Larry Nuttbrock, and Lisa Callahan and Dennis Longmire. Merves shows how a female's body has been traditionally rationalized and made into her nemesis, while Nuttbrock and Callahan and Longmire demonstrate that medical technology not only probes the body, but treats it as a substance.

Second, human action is defined as the movement of matter. Persons are not self-directing, but motivated by subterranean forces that are believed to cause behavior. Abstract physical laws are thus deemed appropriate for evaluating a person's actions. Thus, phenomena such as deviance, illness, normalcy, and health are based on natural principles. This means that behavioral assessments can ignore the existential character of human action and can be conducted in terms of scientific "nosologies."[6] The ways in which technological rationality deanimates medicine, psychiatry, law, and communication are illustrated by Nuttbrock, Callahan and Longmire, John Murphy, David Descutner and DeLysa Burnier, and John Forester.

Third, when conceived technologically, social norms, rules, and laws become abstract. This style of law is sustained by formal rationality, which means that social order is designed to achieve "*impersonal* and *functional* purposes."[7] With this definition, Max

Weber is making a distinction between formal and substantive law. The former represents "calculable rules,"[8] while the latter embodies "ethical imperatives, utilitarian and other expedential rules."[9] In order to avoid personal idiosyncracies and establish a judicial system, order must be severed from questions of ethics. The overall result of this, as Algis Mickunas, John O'Neill, Joseph Freeman, and John Scudder reveal, is that a "technological culture" is promoted that "dehumanizes" political, moral, religious, and aesthetic values.

Fourth, the social imagery that is advanced by a "technological culture" is referred to traditionally as ontological realism. Clearly, this is in tune with the abstract nature of technological rationality.[10] Central to this social ontology is the idea that only an abstract universal can successfully ensure order. Niklas Luhmann, for example, argues that realism portrays society to be "centered."[11] This viewpoint maintains that a reliable base of order cannot be subject to interpretation and thus must exist *sui generis*. Because such a referent resides beyond the domain of language, order is provided with an inviolable ground. Accordingly, social reality is rescued from the melange of competing claims that constitute everyday life. An "ultimate reality," as Talcott Parsons calls it, is thereby available to guarantee social stability.

Ontological realism offers a quantitative or a "measured" image of social order, as norms that represent reality are removed from interpretation.[12] Yet this reality *sui generis* inadvertently reifies the "body politic." Institutionalized order is thus supplied with a seignorial status, while human action is perceived to threaten the rational organization of society. The workplace, as Karen Callaghan and John Murphy and William DiFazio show, begins to resemble an absolute structure that regulates workers' every move.[13] While on the macro level, John O'Neill and Joseph Pilotta and Tim Widman dramatize how such realism tenders the political and communication systems of society impervious to the concerns of citizens.

And fifth, realism results in social development coming to be viewed as following an evolutionary (lawlike) trajectory. Because society exists as an ahistorical monument to order, change is equally nonsocial. As Freeman, Akin Makinde, and Forester demonstrate, social planning is therefore designed to mimic the underlying laws of history when society is perceived technologically. Subsequently, abstract models are invoked to structure space, conceptualize communities, identify a population's traits, and simulate economic and social life. These models, stated simply, are thought to be scientific and thus perfect for engineering social change. Consultants armed with these techniques no longer report a community's sentiments but rather shape its consciousness. These purveyors of political insight are able to do this simply because they are adept at disguising speculation as factual knowledge, as the assumptions of their models go unchallenged due to their alleged scientific stature. Thus, the citizenry is cajoled into performing behavior that is politically, economically, and socially feasible because science is presumed to generate a paucity of errors. Science, in a sense, overwhelms personal judgments and serves to outline the type of unexamined "public opinion" that Auguste Comte claimed would prevent any society from devolving into chaos.

In general, technological rationality creates the illusion that the world is inanimate or similar to the *res extensa* described by Descartes because measurement is substituted for judgment as the proper harbinger of knowledge. Hence, unadulterated reason is juxtaposed with the capriciousness of interpretation, thereby providing the former with immense power. It appears as if technological rationality must struggle to ward off the contaminating effects of the human presence, while preserving truth. As a result, Jacques Ellul writes that technology has become autonomous and specifies what is humanly possible. Technology is perceived to be developing according to the mandates of reasons in order to cleanse the world of uncertainty. Human impulses are thus thought to be disciplined by technological rationality that inadvertently externalizes the locus of control of technology. In this sense, technology is responsible only to its own rationality and erects a particular political economy of truth.

The question that remains to be answered is: How can technology be made responsible to human initiative? In other words, how can technology be humanized? Before technology can be socially responsible, its apparent "affective neutrality" must be challenged, thus shattering its chimera of autonomy[14] As long as technological rationality is treated as pristine and capable of subduing passion, technology will control human destiny. For if humans must adjust to the strictures imposed by technological rationality in order to act reasonably, the autonomy of technology is secure.[15]

A responsible technology, instead, must exhibit "epistemological responsibility." Technological rationality must be understood as a modality of knowledge that emerges from what might be called a "technological unconsciousness," which antedates any application of technological reason. Of key importance is that technological rationality is revealed to be a style of human action, as opposed to the epitome of reason.

Consequently, humanizing technology cannot be viewed as essentially a logistical problem. Merely implementing technology effectively will not necessarily ensure that the human condition is enhanced. Instead, the humanization of technology presupposes self-mastery as opposed to catching a glimpse of pure reason. A responsible technology is a unique "project" of human action. Technological rationality, in short, must be approached as an existential issue for otherwise its social functions will be obscured. The thrust of this collection is to illustrate that technology may become inhumane if its worldview is not thoroughly examined, while technological rationality may provide a ground that will make it socially responsible.

Although a variety of theoretical positions are represented in this volume (phenomenology, Marxism, and critical theory), they have several themes in common that are central to the view of technology presented. First, human action is understood to mediate all knowledge. Accordingly, so-called objective knowledge is replaced by knowledge that is humanly constituted. Second, technology is no longer autonomous because of the claim that it embodies instrumental rationality. This means that technology is merely a modality of reason instead of the paragon of rationality. And third, technology is thus provided with a human ground, thereby placing it in the service of humanity. As a result, technology can further instead of suppress human desires.

What each of these theories does is to deny technology the autonomy that is necessary for it to control social processes. Even though they originate from different intellectual traditions, each theory places human action at the center of history. World development, in this sense, reflects the unfolding of the human spirit. Consequently, technology is not a causal factor in social affairs but an apparatus that needs human action for it to have any purpose and meaning. The "technological imperative" that is allegedly directing social growth is nothing more than a humanly inspired orientation in disguise. This suggests that human aims are able to set the course of history, rather than follow the mandates issued by technological rationality. Nonetheless, before this can happen, human action must be awakened from its present slumber. Each of these theories, additionally, encourages this type of awareness.

By instituting human action as the central metaphysical principle instead of water, air, or some other substance, the measure of all events is no longer abstract. Human understanding, instead, serves as the ultimate judge of any occurrence. What this signals is that the "technological ethic," which provides technology with its legitimacy, is undercut. And in its place is an ethic of human responsibility that assesses all developments in terms of their human or social significance. The measure of technology, therefore, is not technical indicators but the *pathos* that sustains human ambitions. Hence, technology can never deny its human origin, yet the key problem with modern technology is that its human core has been obscured. The theories used in this text are able to correct this difficulty.

NOTES

1. Martin Heidegger, "Die Frage nach der Technik," in *Vortrage und Aufsatz*, Teil 1 (Pfullingen: Verlag Gunther Neske, 1967), p. 20.

2. Daniel Bell, *The Cultural Contradictions of Capitalism* (New York: Basic Books, 1978), pp. 151–154.

3. Eric Voegelin, "Industrial Society in Search of Reason," in Raymond Aron, ed., *World Technology and Human Destiny* (Ann Arbor: University of Michigan Press, 1963), pp. 31–46.

4. Karen A. Callaghan and John W. Murphy, "Premenstrual Syndrome: A Philosophical Exposition," unpublished Manuscript, Arkansas State University, 1984.

5. Max Horkheimer, *Critique of Instrumental Reason* (New York: Seabury Press, 1974), p. vii.

6. Michel Foucault, *The Birth of the Clinic*, trans. A.M. Sheridan Smith (New York: Random House, 1975), p. 104.

7. Max Weber, *Economy and Society*, ed. Guenther Roth and Claus Wittich, vol. 2 (Berkeley: University of California Press, 1978), p. 959.

8. Ibid., p. 975.

9. Max Weber, *Law in Economy and Society*, trans. Edward Shils and Max Rheinstein (Cambridge: Harvard University Press, 1966), pp. 63–64.

10. Peter L. Berger, *Facing up to Modernity* (New York: Basic Books, 1977), p. 21.

11. Niklas Luhmann, *The Differentiation of Society*, trans. Stephen Holmes and Charles Larmore (New York: Columbia University Press, 1982), pp. 353–355.

12. Siegfried Giedion, *Mechanization Takes Command* (New York: W. W. Norton Company, 1969), pp. 49ff.

13. Robert K. Merton, "Bureaucratic Structure and Personality," in Robert K. Merton, Alisa P. Gray, Barbara Hockey, and Hanan C. Selvin, eds., *Reader in Bureaucracy* (New York: Free Press, 1952), pp. 361–371.

14. Peter L. Berger, Brigitte Berger, and Hansfried Kellner, *The Homeless Mind* (New York: Random House, 1973), p. 34.

15. Peter L. Berger, *Pyramids of Sacrifice* (New York: Basic Books, 1974), pp. 166–189.

1

Technological Culture

Algis Mickunas

The task of this essay is to outline the scientific-technological and social worldview present in the modern Western culture. This worldview will be analyzed in terms of the ontology revealed by scientific and political enlightenments. The term "ontology" refers to the assumed structure of social reality and the nature of "man." Additionally, it is shown how the technological worldview fosters a form of government known as technocracy, which stifles democracy and freedom.

SCIENTIFIC ENLIGHTENMENT

The arguments during early Renaissance, advanced by Francis Bacon, Rene Descartes, Isaac Newton, Thomas Hobbes, David Hume, and Gottfried Leibniz, rejected the "old" in favor of the "new" science.[1] The old Aristotelian conception of the world, in which everything had a natural essence and place, was abandoned. Thus, the idea that a qualitative difference exists among things was rejected, along with characteristics such as quality and form. Additionally, the belief emerged that direct observation of natural qualities was not scientific. Yet if the experienced world is irrelevant, what constitutes a "scientific reality"? Stated simply, the view that reality consists of material atoms related in space and time was popularized.[2] Basically, phenomena are sums of material parts whose spatial and temporal movements are related mechanically as cause and effect. When all things are explained in terms of the material parts of which they are composed, an entity is defined solely in terms of its extension, size, weight, and location in space and time.[3] Perceived qualities must be excluded from scientific consideration and are located in the "subject."[4]

This results in the well-known dualism that separates experienced reality, which is subjective, from the "objective" world of science. For, as Leibniz suggests, qualitative characteristics cannot be ascribed to material objects.[5] Thus, science adopts a method that deals with only the presumed objective characteristics of matter, such as in mathematics. The mathematical method disregards differences in quality and treats all things as material objects. What is scientifically valid is not experienced but accessible only through a mathematical method.

The scientific method assumes two attitudes toward nature: indifference and devaluation. If the qualitative distinctions among things are discarded, then phenomena can be treated indifferently. That is, every being can be taken apart and recomposed in any way that is materially possible. Since mathematics measures quantity, material arrangements are the only valid concern of science.

The rejection of experience in favor of the mathematical method essentially devalues nature. Meaning, value, and beauty are ignored as they belong to subjectivity. Nature is meaningless when portrayed as consisting of material parts because human beings give it value and beauty. As Leclerc Buffon points out, brute nature has no beauty. But everything changes only through human action, as beauty flows from the hands of individuals.[6] Nonetheless, three prejudgments characterize the modern age: the devaluation of nature; the elevation of man above nature; and the domination of nature by technological means.

These judgments serve as the basis for the control of nature. Yet as Tilo Schabert states, this requires the transformation of matter in accordance with human designs. For example, Francis Bacon was not motivated by "scientific curiosity," but by his desire to acquire power over nature.[7] Yet complete knowledge of the material processes is necessary for this to occur. If such knowledge is lacking, nature cannot be controlled. Only when all the secrets of nature have been uncovered will individuals be in a position to remake both themselves and nature.[8]

Yet a question arises: What standards should be invoked to guide this process? Clearly not those provided by "human nature" for it also must be redesigned. As a part of the material world, a person is also a set of material parts that can be treated quantitatively. Because there are no essential differences between beings, human nature cannot be viewed as something unique. This is expressed by Pico della Mirandola when he claims that humans were not created according to any standard and thus lack an "intrinsic" nature.[9] That individuals can master and reshape nature, including themselves, is a source of the modern conception of human autonomy.

AUTONOMY AND PRODUCTION

Human autonomy rests not only on a mathematical method but on intervention into nature. Specifically, this method must be applied to nature. This application cannot be simply a mental calculation, for scientists must "test" their mathematical notions by intervening in nature. In other words, matter must be arranged in accordance with mathematical calculations. Once this is completed, persons are in a position to calculate and predict the results that follow from such arrangements. As Karl Heinz Volkmann-Schluck suggests, "reality" is not what is present in human experience, but a possibility that stems from a mathematically calculated and physically manipulated matter.[10]

Thus emerges a structure that treats nature technologically at the most basic level. When taking the mathematical method as the most fundamental mode of theoretical understanding, this style of cognition becomes technological. Mathematical rules not only define nature but prescribe ways of producing the material causes that yield predictable results. In short, to know how to define something mathematically is to know how to make it.[11] In this sense, the application of mathematical constructs becomes a clever technique, as the components of the world are arranged in accordance with certain calculations and the resulting morphology serves as the basis for a technologically conceived world.

This conception places humans "above" nature. In reflective thought, a method is established that excludes the qualitative experience of nature and treats existence as a number of material components that can be arranged mathematically.[12] Mathematics is appropriate for shaping existence because the world is already conceived technologically. The "real world" is thus a product of a reflectively designed theoretical model that shapes matter through calculation.

Hence, scientists are not only in a position to calculate and arrange material conditions to produce predictable results but, conversely, of producing the conditions for attaining these findings. This conversion is one of the major elements of human autonomy and understanding the self as a law giver. But this autonomy cannot be realized unless humans can master nature. After all, as long as persons are controlled by the forces of nature, they cannot be free or autonomous. Nature thus must be forced to function according to human desires.[13] In principle, the mathematical method, combined with the notion that nature is material, establishes the conditions necessary for human autonomy. Humans project desired results and calculate and arrange the material forces required to attain these ends. Nature is made to work in accordance with human designs, as human action dominates the physical world.

It must be pointed out that the projected results do not stem from human nature, for modern thought acknowledges no such phenomenon. Hence, what is projected results from an arrangement of matter that has no intrinsic existence. Therefore, everything, including humans, is treated as "stuff" or "raw material" that can be reworked to meet projected designs. As Eugen Fink points out, scientists intend not only to produce nature in line with preconceived calculations, but above all to "produce man."[14] This leads to the view that persons are a "product" of material conditions. Thus, by projecting material results and producing material conditions, individuals also project and "produce" themselves.

THE POLITICAL ENLIGHTENMENT

While the scientific enlightenment led to the idea that nature is material and "indifferent stuff" to be mastered and controlled, human beings were also permitted to be autonomous and rework nature. This means that humans are in a position to take charge of their destiny. Hence, the traditions that had prescribed norms, moralities, political principles, and ethical standards must be rejected, for all socio-political institutions, which embody laws, must also originate from the individual as law giver.

This calls for political institutions whose sole legitimation depends upon a sum of individuals agreeing to abide by the rules they have established. At base, this is a consensus theory and it takes for granted the equality of all as law givers. This kind of conception of equality is quite revealing, since it demonstrates a shift from the classical Greek tradition. The Greek conception of equality was founded on the understanding that humans share a common nature. Despite their particular differences, humans share an identical essence that makes them equal.[15] Yet characteristically, neither the Greeks nor the Romans under Greek theoretical influence nor, finally, the medievals under the sway of Plato, Aristotle, and Christianity called for practical and socio-political equality.[16]

The demand for socio-political and practical equality emerges when the world is regarded as a material entity to be controlled and shaped according to human design. In terms of this type of equality, persons cannot have laws imposed upon them either by nature or other persons. Hence, equality does not flow from an essential human nature, but from human autonomy. All persons are equal because they are autonomous law givers and makers of their own destiny through their mastery and control of nature. Thus, social institutions must be designed to guarantee human autonomy. This autonomy is expressed in numerous ways: the right of speech, assembly, pursuit of practical aims, and to make one's own destiny.

Martin Kriele suggests that the institutions designed by this political enlightenment take for granted human autonomy as a source of all law. This means, according to him, that no human can assume power over another to gain increased social status. Being autonomous, everyone is an equal source of law, and political institutions represent a consensus among autonomous individuals. As a result, the polity guarantees the rule of law and equality between persons.[17]

It is no accident that the major thinkers of political enlightenment, from John Locke to John Stuart Mill, hold a similar view of political institutions: Laws represent a consensus between free individuals. Contrary to the classical Greek conception of the state as having a human nature and constituting more than a number of isolated individuals, modern theorists take for granted that society is the sum of individual interests. Thus, laws reflect the ways individuals agree to interact with one another. Since a complete consensus is rarely attained, quantitative power prevails: The numerical majority constitutes a temporary "rule" with the proviso that the minority has the right to persuade the majority to change. As Martin Kriele suggests, the only right that political institutions do not permit is the abolition of human autonomy.[18]

Accordingly, a specifically modern conception of ethics comes into view: utilitariansim. In this case, each individual defines what is meant by the "good life." Basically, the good life consists of the pursuit of happiness and pleasure. As long as these pursuits do not create social clashes and antagonisms, individuals are free to design their own happiness. In case of conflicts, the social good is calculated quantitatively as the greatest good for the greatest number. This numerical conception of happiness accords well with a technologically conceived world. Yet the question arises: What constitutes happiness in a technologically produced reality?

TECHNOLOGICAL AIMS: POWER AND POSSESSION

To control nature and change its course of development demands extensive technological power. As Hans Jonas argues, modern society believes that every technological innovation and application leads to new "discoveries" that call for newer technologies and their application in an endless cycle. Yet every new technological intervention into nature promises increased control of both nature and humans. This is the "enchanted circle" of the modern man.[19] Every achieved result can become a means, that is, a material condition for the fulfillment of newer aims. Nowadays, this is called "progress."[20]

The increasing power to control nature and to reproduce it in accordance with human designs expands the material fulfillment of human wants. Such fulfillment has assumed a particularly modern form. A brief comparison between two conceptions of fulfillment illustrates this point. In feudalism, a person was born into a particular social position. To be an aristocrat, one had to be ascribed this status by birth. The same was true of the serf. Of course, the serf's birthright excluded any hope of being an aristocrat. But with the emergence of the demand for equality, founded upon the idea of the human as an autonomous law giver, all positions become available to everyone. All persons can make themselves into anything they desire. Yet it must be noted that this self-production operates within a technological culture whose main aim is to submit nature to human controls and to liberate persons by giving them increased technical power.

When persons make their own destiny, they must also guarantee their own well-being. No social institution, position, or privilege is able to ensure an individual's survival. Because each position is open to everyone, persons must strive constantly to maintain their social position. In fact, such a striving can never cease in a technological culture.[21] Initially, increased control over nature seems to be a panacea because more commodities, protection against the elements, and control of disease offer hope for improving the material conditions of existence. Yet it is this miracle of increased power and possessions that brings about insecurity and compels individuals to acquire more power in the form of material objects.

As is suggested, technology has no other aim but to master nature through the ever-increasing materialization of culture. On the basis of technological innovations, new and more complex technologies are produced that make the previous ones obsolete. As a result, persons who were functioning adequately within the framework supplied by earlier technological requirements, that is, they were "tooled" appropriately, become either obsolete or must strive to "retool" themselves in order to keep up with the demands of technology and ensure their survival. Since a technological conception of the world has no other aim but "progress" through expansion, no individual can ever be satisfied with his or her own level of technological sophistication. Persons must strive constantly to keep up with the ever-increasing and changing technological requirements. In principle, security can never be achieved, for at best persons can only minimize the danger of becoming obsolete and losing their means of survival.

In order to achieve a modicum of security, individuals must acquire not only the skills demanded by technology, but, additionally, material possessions. Happiness is equated with material commodities, not because their possession serves as a testimonial to human greed, but because, in a technological culture, they are thought to promote well-being. By amassing wealth, one guards against the threat of personal or social destruction. Even those who have achieved a particular status due to their expertise in some technical domain can lose their possessions. They must concentrate on maintaining their "competitive edge" or "technological competence," which is always threatened by the progress made by others toward mastering more advanced technologies. The desire to possess more as a road to happiness is ultimately a desire to attain security, not only for the present but also for the future. After all, all current possessions can be lost as a consequence of advances brought about by novel technologies. In order to avoid this loss, the future must be remade constantly by better or more efficient machinery so that any losses are minimized. While this is the source for the charge that the modern age is materialistic, a subtle shift away from human autonomy is also signaled.

In order to function in a technological culture, an individual must be made to operate according to the requirements of constantly expanding and changing technologies. The ability to acquire possessions requires that the individual submit to the dictates and aims of technology. Persons must not "make" themselves in terms of what they value and desire, but according to the strictures imposed by technology. The mastered nature, shaped into technological implements and raw material and designed initially to "liberate" persons from natural forces, has come to shape humans. Instead of being autonomous, individuals begin to regard themselves, at least in the practical arena, as a "product" of their socio-economic and technical environment.

At the base of this shift away from autonomy lies the notion that persons can shape anything to obtain a desired result and can remake themselves because they have no nature. Yet this also means that humans can be made into anything. The claim is often made that, given certain conditions, a person can be given practically any form. This is obvious considering the common feature in most modern social, psychological, and economic theories: An individual is a result or product of his or her socio-economic and environmental conditions. In this sense, the socio-economic and technological conditions assume a "life of their own," thus compelling the individual to function within or adjust to fit the requirements of the technical system. This would suggest that the technological system has become autonomous, thereby diminishing the individual.

POLITICAL TECHNOCRACY

Individual autonomy, political enlightenment, and the scientific enlightenment, which form the cornerstone of technological culture, are undergoing a transformation that has resulted in what Jurgen Habermas calls a "legitimation crisis."[22] While Habermas assesses this crisis in terms of the capitalist economy, a more expansive approach examines what the critical school refers to as the domination of human creativity by "instrumental reason."[23] Such rationality is basically the technological logic depicted above. The crisis appears in two forms of the polity. The liberal form of state, characteristic of Western industrial societies, experiences this crisis as the "privatization" of political institutions. While initially these institutions were designed to serve the public, gradually they were reduced to promoting the personal or material well-being of citizens. For if the basic aim of the individual in a technological culture is the acquisition of possessions, then the emphasis of political life must be to get public figures to ensure the material well-being of persons. Subsequently, politicians are called upon increasingly to fulfill the material needs of the citizenry or to do whatever it takes to prepare individuals to meet the demands imposed by new technologies. Any time they fail to fulfill these needs, politicians are no longer deemed legitimate and they are replaced. Thus, political institutions are regarded as means to be appropriated and used by contesting groups to guarantee their material fulfillment. As the saying goes, political concerns are reduced to "pocketbook" issues. The other form of state, nominally called "communism," takes "instrumental reason," or "technological logic," to its final conclusion. Stated simply, everything is either a technical means or a result of a technologically shaped world. In this sense, humans are treated as both a means for constructing the material conditions necessary for technological progress and a product of these circumstances. Such products are not only predicated on knowledge about material conditions but, conversely, conditions can be established that yield a particular result. Fundamentally, this represents an effort to build a utopian society conceived technologically. To build such a state and to "create" the "new man" appropriate for this polity, calls for a "political technocracy."

What is the function of a political technocracy in the current historical period? First, since the claim is made that everything, including human consciousness and social institutions, is a product of material conditions, then the establishment of new conditions would be necessary to bring about future institutions. Second, since these institutions are the result of material conditions, those who know these conditions and how to change them for a "better" future must be free from institutional restraints. Most often, it is understood that scientific and technological complexities are not accessible to the general public. Hence, there must be a political technocracy with the knowledge necessary to establish the material conditions that would result in a radically new, utopian society. Such a technocracy must be able to redesign the material processes in every area of social life. And third, this political technocracy must consist of elites who are in charge of planning the future. Since the current material conditions are not yet adequate for realizing a utopia, these elites must not be hindered by political institutions that stress human freedom. Only when the proper material conditions are established will "true liberation" of humanity be possible because science must be able to master nature, including the human side of life.[24]

These political elites, armed with scientific knowledge, have a historical mission to use all the available means, including humans, to achieve the desired free society. But with this there appears an undemocratic form of "leadership," because allegedly only a few persons have the scientific knowledge required to shape the social world. These leaders are the only autonomous beings and outlive the destiny of entire populations. The liberation and autonomy of the masses is postponed until the political technocrats have established the appropriate conditions for creating the new man.[25]

In principle, the political trend toward technocracy and "material fulfillment" is a sign that politics is being surrendered to the scientific-technological enlightenment and its promise to liberate society. This can be seen as an effort to fulfill the promise of two enlightenments: complete human autonomy and mastery over every facet of the environment. Since these promises have not yet been fulfilled, the modern age is caught between two histories.[26] Although at different levels, both histories are implicit in each other's development. The first history understands humans to be "self-creating" and autonomous beings, who not only create themselves—having no specific nature—but reduce nature to matter and recreate the environment. The second history represents the attempt to realize the first. Such efforts inhere to technological progress and procurement of technical power. Since the mastery of nature has not yet been achieved, the first history has been postponed and projected toward the future as a utopian society. Its realization consists of a struggle by a scientifically enlightened political technocracy to use any means possible to bring about a technologically constructed polity.

CONCLUSION

Not everyone looks favorably at the promise of increased mastery over nature and society. There appears to be a growing mistrust of the ability of technicians to "solve the riddle of history." Technological solutions have resulted in unsuspected and negative consequences leading to a vicious developmental cycle.[27] To solve these unsuspected results, more technology has to be introduced and thus more unforeseen problems occur that can be remedied only by more technology, meaning that technological solutions become a part of the problem. Yet within a context of a technological culture, that such solutions are the only ones available as a technocratic consciousness is self-propagating. Accordingly, the political technocracy is also enhanced. After all, it must solve the public hazards created by technology. In this sense, the political power of technocrats must also grow. The growth of political technocracy eventually concentrates political power in the hands of "experts," who have the technological expertise to control the processes necessary to fulfill human needs. Thus, political power turns into material power as political institutions become the media whereby material favors and guarantees of well-being are distributed on the basis of political affiliations. This cynical consciousness appears among those political functionaries who know that their final aim is no longer "liberation through science" but the acquisition of power.[28] The major concern of politics becomes the maintenance of the technological edge that sustains power.

Any serious solution to the dilemmas proposed by a technologically conceived world must abandon instrumental reason as an appropriate *modus operandi*. Alternatives exist, as illustrated by the ability of persons to solve problems without technocrats. This experience provides individuals with a "lived world" that, while overlooked by instrumental reason, exists for even the most ardent technocrat. While human, ambiguous, and historically contingent, the lived world provides a network of relationships that cannot be reduced to a set of mathematical points. Additionally, this world lends purpose and meaning even to the world of science, as illustrated in the conclusion of this collection. The lived world can provide insight into solving many of the problems posed by technology because instrumental reason is shown to be an outgrowth of human experience. When this is the case, technology is provided with a human context and illustrated to be based on values that must not be overlooked when it is used. Thus, humans are able to give technology direction instead of being enslaved by its demands.

NOTES

1. Tilo Schabert, *Gewalt und Humanitaet* (Frieburg/Muenchen: Verlag Karl Alber, 1978), p. 65.

2. Kurt Lasswitz, *Geschichte der Atomistik vom Mittelalter bis Newton*, (Darmstadt: Wissenschaftliche Buchgesellschaft, 1963), p. 124.

3. Ibid., p. 141.

4. Algis Mickunas, "Essence of the Technological World," in Lester Embree, ed., *Essays in Memory of Aron Gurwitsch* (Washington, D.C.: University Press of America, 1984, p. 100.

5. Gottfried W. Leibniz, *Neue Abhandlungen ueber den menschlichen Verstand* (Frankfurt am Main: Insel Verlag, 1961), p. 205.

6. Schabert, *Gewalt und Humanitaet*, p. 107.

7. Ibid., p. 141.

8. Ibid., p. 142.

9. Ibid., p. 39.

10. Karl H. Volkmann-Schluck, *Einfuehrung in das philosophische Denken* (Frankfurt am Main: Vittorio Klostermann, 1965), p. 68.

11. Ibid., p. 66.

12. Edmund Husserl, *Cartesianische Meditationen und Pariser Vortraege* (Den Haag: Martinus Nijhoff, 1963), p. 179.

13. Volkmann-Schluck, *Einfuehrung in das philosophische Denken*, p. 68.

14. Eugen Fink, *Traktat ueber die Gewalt des Menschen* (Frankfurt am Main: Vittorio Klostermann, 1974), p. 41.

15. Karl H. Volkmann-Schluck, *Politische Philosophie* (Frankfurt am Main: Vittorio Klostermann, 1974), p. 152.

16. Ibid., p. 154.

17. Martin Kriele, *Befreiung und Politische Aufklaerung* (Freiburg: Herder Verlag, 1980), p. 49.

18. Ibid., p. 190.

19. Fink, *Traktat ueber die Gewalt des Menschen*, p. 43.

20. Hans Jonas, "Philosophisches zur modernen Technologie," in Reinhard Loew, ed., *Fortschritt ohne Mass* (Muenchen: Piper & Co. Verlag, 1981), p. 81.

21. Volkmann-Schluck, *Politische Philosophie*, p. 164.

22. Jurgen Habermas, *Legitimationsprobleme im Spaetkapitalismus* (Frankfurt am Main: Suhrkamp Verlag, 1973), p. 43.

23. Thomas McCarthy, *The Critical Theory of Jurgen Habermas* (Cambridge: M.I.T. Press, 1978), p. 16.

24. Kriele, *Befreiung und Politische Aufklaerung*, p. 204.

25. Michael Albert and Robin Hahnel, *Socialism Today and Tomorrow* (Boston: South End Press, 1981), p. 77

26. Schabert, *Gewalt und Humanitaet*, p. 225

27. Langdon Gilkey, "The Religious Dilemmas of a Scientific Culture: The Interface of Technology, History and Religion," in David Stewart and Donald Borchert, eds., *Being Human in a Technological Age* (Athens: Ohio University Press, 1979), p. 78.

28. Peter Sloterdijk, *Kritik der Zynischen Vernunft* (Frankfurt am Main: Suhrkamp Verlag, 1983), p. 37.

2

Changes in Technological Social Control: Theory and Implications for the Workplace

Karen A. Callaghan and John W. Murphy

This chapter is motivated by a recently published book that deals inadequately with the impact technology has had on removing the control of the workplace from workers.[1] There are three key reasons for this book's failure. First, too much time is spent on the influence of Frederick Taylor. Second, no mention is made of how the use of technology as a means of social control has changed over the years. And third, no discussion is offered about how the most modern version of technology, that is, the self-equilibrating machine, has added an ontological dimension to this control issue that was missing from earlier periods. To correct these difficulties, this presentation assumes a particular form. Specifically, the various key conceptions of technology, their respective images of the workplace, and how they each understand social control is discussed.

THE SOCIAL TECHNOLOGY OF FREDERICK TAYLOR

Taylor developed "scientific management" as a replacement for what he calls "ordinary management" in order to alleviate the chaos he witnessed in the workplace. He believes this disorder stemmed from the rule-of-thumb measures that were being used to regulate work.[2] In opposition to these, Taylor hoped to discover the one best way for structuring the workplace, thereby promoting harmony. He modeled the rules used to design work in accordance with the scientific procedures extolled by engineers. Taylor believes these are sound principles that could be used to organize the workplace rationally.

As Harry Braverman points out, scientific management represents a technological means to control the workplace.[3] This approach to social organization is considered technological simply because science dictates how work is to be performed.[4] Each of Taylor's innovations is aimed at removing, or limiting as far as possible, the influence of subjectivity (or the human element) from the work process. For a variety of reasons, he thought this would improve conditions at the workplace. First, work goals would be scientifically (objectively) outlined. Second, the quality of work could be measured quantitatively. And third, discipline could be enforced through scientific job design. Accordingly, Taylor believes that scientific management would be an effective method of social control because the workplace could be designed with precision.

Nevertheless, Taylorism did not prove to be as effective as originally anticipated for securing order and actually generated discord among workers. This occurred, as Henri Fayol suggests, because Taylor did not conceive of the workplace as an administrative machine.[5] Specifically, Taylor built his view of the workplace from the ground up, and therefore its structure appears to have a finite character. Because the workplace is not portrayed as existing *sui generis*, the design of work seemed arbitrary, with particular groups receiving more benefits than others. In fact, Taylor believes that managers should plan the work process, while workers perform only the simplest tasks. Therefore, scientific management came to be understood as a tool used by managers to control workers as workers began to view their freedom as systematically curtailed by this style of organization.

Scientific management, stated simply, did not advance an all-encompassing social ontology and because of this was perceived as a means of organizational control. Gradually, Taylorism became viewed as inhumane because workers were reduced to a machinelike existence and stripped of their dignity.[6] The controversy over the repressive nature of scientific management culminated in Taylor having to testify before a special House Committee, impaneled to inquire into the possible misuse of this organizational strategy. Around 1915, the popularity of Taylorism began to wane because the disruptive effects of scientific management began to overshadow its ability to secure order.

This is not to suggest that technological strategies of social control were abandoned but more efficient ones had to be discovered. Stated simply, the source of legitimation for technological social control must become more universal or it will always be assessed as unfair and create social strife. Since a social ontology cannot exist *sui generis* if it is derived inductively, a conception of order must be invoked that does not have a contingent origin.[7] In view of this criticism, scientific management represents a fairly crude method of technological control because the rules that regulate the workplace are particularistic and require direct intervention into the workplace to secure order.

THREE TRADITIONAL TECHNOLOGICAL ONTOLOGIES: ATTEMPTS AT A SYSTEM

Following the decline of Taylorism, a variety of approaches was tried for organizing the workplace. Their general aim is to be universalistic, so that social order represents a system. Using Parsonian terminology, the workplace must no longer be structured in terms of situational exigencies but in terms of an "ultimate reality."[8] Like Plato's ideas or Aristotle's primal matter, this reality becomes the progenitor of all that exists, including the workplace. Social control, therefore, is understood as promoting the overall security of the workplace and not merely the particular interests of select persons.

EMILE DURKHEIM: THE DIVISION OF LABOR

In his debate with the ghost of Immanuel Kant and the utilitarians, Emile Durkheim argues that a firm moral order can only be established on a reality *sui generis* as opposed to individual judgments. These collective sentiments do not necessarily remain static but change over time. For example, as societies become more complex, the rules of moral conduct assume a form that is different from earlier periods. Yet their purpose is always the same: to provide a universal base of social order.[9]

A rigorous division of labor is one means of generating social control. As the division of labor develops, persons become increasingly specialized and separated from those around them, thus resulting in what Jean-Paul Sartre calls "serialization."[10] For when the workplace is fragmented, it is simultaneously atomized as the illusion is created that each person (or task) constitutes a self-contained unit. Durkheim argues that this is an adequate method of social control because it is predicated upon mutual dependence among persons that is regulated by rules that exist *sui generis*. Simply put, workers who are specialized to the extent that they have minimal knowledge of the production process are controlled by a system they cannot comprehend.

Durkheim's argument is that work cannot be regulated effectively by merely adjusting individuals to specific tasks but, more important, sound explanations must be offered about the organization of these tasks. And according to him, when conceived as a reality *sui generis*, the workplace can be coordinated effectively without portraying workers as manipulated by those in power. Differences in power do not appear to benefit only a small group of persons but the workplace as a whole. The workplace, stated simply, is perceived to have a general orientation that prescribes how all jobs should be operationalized.[11]

Yet the question remains: Is Durkheim successful in creating what Herbert Marcuse calls a "one dimensional" view of social reality? Is Durkheim able to show that the structure of the workplace embodies a *mathesis universalis*? Taylor's inability to do this brought about the eventual demise of his model of the workplace as its organization seemed arbitrary and, thus, oppressive. If Durkheim's method of control is to advance beyond Taylor's *modus operandi*, this problem must be sufficiently remedied.

Although Durkheim states repeatedly that social structure does not reflect "conventional or arbitrary arrangements," he does not necessarily identify it with a monistic source.[12] He contends that happiness results from a proper alignment of the individual to structural demands.[13] Yet the procedure whereby this is accomplished is not clear, thus jeopardizing the isomorphism between workers and their roles. While using Gottfried Leibniz's phrase, Durkheim suggests that a "preexisting harmony" exists between the individual and social structure without ever demonstrating how this occurs. In fact, his identification of the individual with organizational imperatives is replete with conflict.

For instance, Durkheim argues that a natural attraction exists between persons and their proper location in a division of labor based on a type of pleasure principle. Is Durkheim invoking a thesis similar to that offered by Jeremy Bentham and John Stuart

Mill? Certainly not, for he distrusts their utilitarianism. Instead, he cites the work of E. H. Weber and Gustav Fechner and declares that pleasure represents a nervous vibration that is neither too weak nor exceedingly intense.[14] Also, Durkheim refers obliquely to the existence of a normative physiological response that is indicative of acceptable behavior. Finally, he admits that he cannot be exact and describes the state that humans strive to maintain as equilibrium.

Durkheim says that this physiological state can be corroborated by experience. Nonetheless, the states that the causal relationship between individual desires and social structure "can never be anything but imperfect and proximate."[15] In fact, he begins to speak aimlessly about the solidarity, conflict, and cohesion (resemblance) that accompany structural differentiation as his discussion devolves into a morass of conflicting claims. Whereas originally a reality *sui generis* is identified as reconciling all social differences, this position is replaced by obscure physiological theses that rest on unclarified philosophical principles.[16] As a result, Durkheim has a difficult time justifying job assignments and supplying a sound rationale for social control.

THE HUMAN RELATIONS SCHOOL: A MANAGERIAL ELITE

The second ontology that attempts to improve upon Taylorism also relies on the work of Durkheim in addition to Vilfredo Pareto. This is the ontology advanced by the human relations school. The holistic social imagery adopted by this position was available to Taylor but was mostly unused. Specifically, the machine analogy presupposed by Taylor is brought to the forefront to describe how the components of the workplace should be arranged. It is assumed that each facet of the workplace has a distinct task to perform in terms of maintaining this organization. The machine (or workplace) delimits the function (existence) of each of its parts yet is not implicated in their contingent nature. This style of thinking results in an ontological ground that legitimizes individual existence because it is immune to situational exigencies. However, do these human relations theorists detail successfully how this version of the workplace merges the individual and the organization?

Elton Mayo claims that the modern workplace is in a state of "anomie." Accordingly, he argues that a sense of collective responsibility must be instilled in the citizenry. For this to occur, however, a collective spirit must be engendered among persons. Yet Mayo and his human relations colleagues are not successful in this endeavor.

Mayo laments the passage of what he calls a "functional society," a type of *Gemeinschaft*.[17] Because the modern world is so complex, he contends that it is very difficult for persons to know explicitly how they fit into its grand design. To rectify this problem, Mayo invokes solutions that stress the need to educate citizens to understand their social responsibility. For as Mayo states, the establishment of society cannot be left to chance, which is a theme also echoed by Durkheim.[18]

The human relations authors employ the principle of equilibrium espoused by Pareto to describe how work should be structured.[19] Yet when portrayed as a machine, society equilibrates around a norm that is merely presupposed. Most important is how this norm is given legitimacy. Initially, the work of Quesnay is applauded, for Mayo suggests that he discovered natural laws for regulating the workplace.[20] Later, Mayo abandons François Quesnay because he was too vague about these laws. R. H. Tawney's idea that morality can be taught is mentioned next, yet it is not really given serious consideration. Bronislaw Malinowski is also cited briefly as arguing that the individual can be subordinated humanely to the social whole. Finally, Jean Piaget is recognized as offering evidence that social morality is a product of education. Yet none of these theories are ever fully explored.

Without sufficient development of any of these themes, Mayo states that a managerial elite must operate the workplace in order to avoid anomie. Because Pareto is credited for this proposal, the asymmetry present in the social world is hardly reduced. Instead, Mayo simply reinforces the traditional notion that workers should be controlled by an elite corps of planners. Thus, organizational power is portrayed particularistically and social asymmetry is given legitimacy. Therefore, this procedure of social control does not improve upon Taylor's because order still does not emerge from a universal ground.

MAX WEBER: COSMOLOGICAL ORGANIZATION

Another traditional form of technological control is discussed by Max Weber. Although not a proponent of bureaucracy, Weber gives a clear description of its ontological character. He argues that bureaucracy is considered desirable because it is sustained by formal reason and portrays the world as "impersonal."[21] When based on formal reason, the world is divorced from human valuation and provides an abstract (universal) referent for order. Accordingly, administrative decisions can be made according to logic that is treated as unequivocal, thus promoting the image of a smoothly running organization.

Weber refers to this as the increasing rationalization of the world, as values are systematically replaced by logic that is believed to be unencumbered by human contingencies. The resulting organization, he declares, fosters a spirit of "formalistic impersonality," as all persons are "levelled" to a common denominator.[22] As a result of increasing formalism, administrative arbitrariness is reduced because personal privileges do not affect decision making. Organizations appear to exist *sui generis* because they are severed from substantive rationality. Organizations attain what Lucien Goldmann calls a tragic status, for they resemble a monolithic edifice and cannot be challenged. For this reason, Weber calls bureaucracy an "iron cage."

Thus far, Weber has not said anything different from Durkheim. The formal reason discussed by Weber is similar to Durkheim's reality *sui generis*. However, Weber provides a much more developed theory of how an individual is aligned to an organization. Weber mentions first that a bureaucracy is driven by a "spirit," which carries Hegelian overtones. Yet he does not pursue this argument but rather uses Lutheran imagery to describe how persons are assigned jobs in organization. Weber uses the word *beruf*, or calling, to refer to an occupation, thereby providing the workplace with a *telos* that guides individuals to their respective positions in this organization.[23] All persons are reconciled to their proper social roles and organizational harmony secured as history unfolds because a heteronomous source of order structures the workplace and ensures persons are placed in appropriate jobs.

Weber's thesis is the most complete view of organizational control discussed thus far. He argues successfully that the workplace exists *sui generis*, that its base is impersonal and universal, and that workers are organized by a cosmological-like *telos*. Accordingly, Weber's theory is better than those proffered by Taylor, Durkheim, and the human relations writers as it creates a total system of control.

Weber's rendition of technological control is much more difficult to overcome than those previously posed because control is not structural, physical, or psychological but ontological. Therefore, control is not an outgrowth of a particular force, or *modis operandi*, but a conception of social (organizational) reality that diminishes the importance of human action. Because the structure of the workplace embodies reason, persons are considered to be rational only when they mimic structural objectives. And because human action is stripped of its valuative capacity, persons are conceived as passive.

Because this style of organizational control diminishes human action indirectly, merely attacking organizations will not guarantee human freedom. Although this is typically the response of those who want to prevent technology from controlling the workplace, human action is not necessarily liberated from organizational domination. For organizational hegemony can be eliminated only if the workplace is provided with a concrete ground, one based on human action.

Even though Weber ostensibly describes a mode of social order that is divorced from human contingency and, thus, inviolable, a problem exists with his rhetoric. Stated simply, Weber's rendition of bureaucratic (technological) control is too metaphysical and thus speculative. Thus, the absolute ontological (cosmological) ground he posits is compromised because social actors are provided implicitly with the latitude to think critically about their origin. Due to his introduction of metaphysics, a potentially closed system is suddenly riddled with ambiguity and open to question.

SYSTEMS THEORY AND MODERN TECHNOLOGICAL CONTROL

Early on, Frederick Pollock noted that cybernetics introduced a new dimension to the discussion of organizational control.[24] Because newer machines are self-directing, or self-equilibrating, he argues that they seem to have a foreboding sense of autonomy. Since machines can be programmed to direct themselves due to "feedback," they are also self-correcting. As a result, machines can be perceived as having a purpose (or *telos* in Weberian terms) that is not necessarily a metaphysical or final cause. This means that organizations can be understood as autonomous and yet not metaphysical because all directives are provided "here and now" and not in terms of an eternal plan. As Max Horkheimer says, systems thinking represents the most complete attack on metaphysics yet devised, for it rules out speculation and provides institutions with a substantive yet autonomous form.[25] As a strategy for ensuring order, this scenario establishes an intractable system of technological social control because organizations appear to have an imminent sense of direction.

Yet it remains to be shown how this nonspeculative organizational autonomy is justified theoretically. Thus, the work of Talcott Parsons must be consulted, for he demonstrates clearly how a sociological systems (cybernetic) theory works. Before this discussion can proceed, two key points must be mentioned about systems theory. First, mature systems are arranged in a hierarchy and, second, the information that guides a system resides at its highest level, while the energy required to animate a system is discovered at the bottom.[26] As Parsons reveals, when invoked simultaneously, these two principles guarantee the autonomy of a social system without introducing unverifiable ideas.

For example, human energy is located at the lower end of a cybernetic hierarchy and has no innate direction.[27] This energy represents merely crude potential until it is given form, which originates from a source higher in the cybernetic system. Because information is placed at the apex of this hierarchy, it has the power to shape energy and give it direction. Most important is that energy (a human product) does not have an orientation until it is joined with information and thus receives an identity *ex post facto*. As a result, the only identity human beings have is prescribed by the social system, since only it can supply the information necessary for making energy socially meaningful.

Since personal identities are realized only after they are sanctioned by the higher levels of the social system, they can only assume a form that the system imprints. This results in a one-dimensional world because only the knowledge that is imparted by the system is available. All other types of information are treated as irrational because they do not resemble this particular form of reason. Eventually, the social system is treated as ultimately real for it cannot be reflected upon critically. In fact, the knowledge that represents the system can only be "copied" (as discussed by Vladimir Lenin) as closely as possible, as knowledge acquisition is a mimetic act. Subsequently, the dominance of the social system is guaranteed since the individuals are subordinate to its demands.

Clearly this is a more comprehensive method of ensuring social order than those adopted in the past because the origin of control is a structure that all individuals must introject if they are to have an identity. Hence, an organization resembles an unquestionably real phenomenon, a natural force that serves as the standard bearer of reason. This is why this style of technological control is thought to regulate existence from the "here and now," although the norms that control the workplace are presumed to exist *sui generis*. Nonetheless, persons come to believe that they are facing an intractable edifice that cannot be transcended except by risking one's sanity. As Ernst Bloch suggests, this type of world is devoid of hope because human action cannot find expression. Literally, this world is closed because it is naively accepted as real.

During the period from the early 1950s to the mid–1960s, systems theory dominated the American management scene as a solution to the perennial problem of merging the individual with the organization.[28] By using systems theory, individualism can be encouraged while the organization (or system) assumes its traditional seignorial role. This type of association is possible because of a theoretical technicality that stipulates that individuals cannot feel oppressed unless their desires are blocked. Since personal and organizational demands are considered synonymous in systems theory, individualism is tolerated but only within the strictures imposed by the system. This is an ideal system of control simply because all persons must adopt the system's definition of freedom if they are to have an identity.

Clearly this method of social control is difficult to combat because it results from a tightly woven ontological argument. As Michel Foucault indicates, when social structures embody reason and human action is anti-reason unless it mimics structurally outlined modes of behavior, the only available policy is to diminish personal experiences. Suddenly, as Don Idhe declares, the world is "deanimated" and, as suggested by both Maurice Merleau-Ponty and Niklas Luhmann, individuals can no longer provide social life with direction and meaning. Accordingly, life becomes merely a process whereby human beings adjust to structural constraints. Life is an endless attempt to master techniques as they dictate how and under what conditions work is to be conducted.

Jacques Ellul calls this "technological slavery," for social action is divorced from human control.[29] A similar point is made by Martin Heidegger when he states that modern technology has been given immense power because it has lost all contact with its human ground.[30] Edmund Husserl makes a similar argument when he suggests that only because science denies any connection with the *lebenswelt*, or "lifeworld," is it thought to be superior to subjectivity.[31] Technocrats follow a similar tack by identifying technology with reason (*ultimia ratio*), while other forms of human expression are given a lesser ontological status. Technological rationality, therefore, is envisaged to penetrate to the core of life, rooting out all irrational forms of thinking. Modern technology arrogates to itself an unassailable position, as reason cannot be challenged effectively by nonreason. Technology *qua* reason, therefore, is able to dominate the social scene.

Modern technology offers the most rigorous model of social control possible. Because technological rationality serves as its own progenitor, the world can be arranged as it sees fit. And because of the ontological nature of this argument, this form of social control is qualitatively different from those of the past as they use relatively crude structural means to secure order. While structural modes of control confront an individual and exact conformity through intimidation, they still presuppose that human actors are capable of self-determination. This is not the case with modern technology, as control results from subverting individual action through an ontological argument.

Modern technology destroys the force of opposition by reducing human action to irrationality. The result of this is not a direct or imposing form of control, but the results are the same—that is, objectivity dominates subjectivity (human action) and erects an asymmetrical mode of order. Foucault refers to this as "terrorizing" human action into submission by ontological forces although in an allegedly nonviolent manner.

This is not to suggest a type of technological determinism whereby workers cannot challenge social order but to indicate that direct assaults on this means of control are not sufficient for human liberation. More important, a sense of theoretical maturity must be fostered that sublates the separation of reason from nonreason so that human action cannot be deprived of its ability to be self-determining. For, as Foucault suggests, only through such theorizing can the power of technological rationality be undercut and human *praxis* set free.

CONCLUSION

This need for improved theoretical sophistication poses new challenges for those who want to undercut the imperial nature of modern technology. As Edward Ballard suggests, Socratic questions that pertain to the character of the self must be asked before any serious criticism of technology can be offered.[32] By proceeding this way, moreover, human action can be resurrected to ground technology, so that it can be used responsibly. Without posing this existential question of technology, its grip on humankind cannot be loosened. For if technology is to foster social self-determination, it must be sustained by human action or it will remain an impenetrable mode of control. As long as technological rationality can claim immunity to existential questions, it will rule its creators.

The hegemony of modern technology can be subverted only by illustrating that all phenomena are mediated by human action. Subsequently, technology is returned to the interhuman lifeworld and understood to be a modality of existential expression, as suggested by Husserl. When viewed this way, technology cannot be a heteronomous tool of social control because it can never have the ontological status needed for this role. Yet until a human ground of technology is established, the prevailing autonomous image of the workplace cannot be undercut.[33]

NOTES

1. Stephen Wood, ed., *The Degradation of Work?* (London: Hutchinson, 1982).

2. Frederick W. Taylor, *Principles of Scientific Management* (New York: Harper and Row, 1911), pp. 36–37.

3. Harry Braverman, *Labor and Monopoly Capital* (New York: Monthly Review Press, 1974), pp. 90ff.

4. The images of the workplace offered by Taylor, Durkheim, the human relations School, and Weber are technological in the broadest sense of the term. That is, they are divorced from human expression, are considered to be structurally objective, are mechanistic, and are sustained by what is believed to be formalized reason. A high-tech version of the workplace does not arise until the introduction of cybernetics into management theory. For a discussion of this type of definition, consult Hans Lenk, "Technokratie und Technologie: Notizen zu einer ideological Diskussion," in Hans Lenk, ed., *Technokratie als Ideologie* (Stuttgart: Verlag W. Kohlhammer, 1973), pp. 105–124.

5. Henri Fayol, *General and Industrial Management*, trans. Constance Storrs (New York: Pittman Publishing, 1949), p. 57.

6. Georges Friedmann, *Industrial Society*, trans. Harold L. Sheppard (Glencoe, Ill.: Free Press, 1961), pp. 41ff.

7. Georges Friedmann, *The Anatomy of Work*, trans. Wyatt Rawson (New York: Free Press, 1961), p. 33.

8. Talcott Parsons, *Societies: Evolutionary and Comparative Perspectives* (Englewood Cliffs, N.J.: Prentice-Hall, 1966), p. 28.

9. Emile Durkheim, *The Division of Labor*, trans. George Simpson (Glencoe, Ill.: Free Press, 1960), p. 61.

10. Jean-Paul Sartre, *Life/Situations*, trans. Paul Auster and Lydia Davis (New York: Pantheon Books, 1977), pp. 167ff.

11. Emile Durkheim, *The Rules of Sociological Method*, trans. Sarah A. Solovay and John H. Mueller (New York: Free Press, 1966), pp. 110–111.

12. Ibid., p. 123.

13. Durkheim, *The Division of Labor*, p. 249.

14. Ibid., p. 235.

15. Ibid., p. 275.

16. Ibid., p. 279.

17. Elton Mayo, *The Human Problems of an Industrial Civilization* (Boston: Macmillan, 1946), pp. 138–160.

18. Elton Mayo, "Foreword," in F. J. Roethlisberger, *Management and Morale* (Cambridge: Harvard University Press, 1942), p. xix.

19. Roethlisberger, *Management and Morale*, p. 185.

20. Mayo, *Human Problems of an Industrial Civilization*, pp. 140–141.

21. Max Weber, *Law and Economy in Society*, trans. Edward Shils and Max Rheinstein (Cambridge: Harvard University Press, 1966), pp. 278ff.

22. Max Weber, *Social and Economic Organization*, trans. A.M. Henderson and Talcott Parsons (New York: Macmillan, 1947), p. 340.

23. Ibid., p. 250.

24. See Frederick Pollock, *The Economic and Social Consequences of Automation* (Oxford: Basil Blackwell, 1957), passim.

25. Max Horkheimer, "The Latest Attack on Metaphysics," in Horkheimer, *Critical Theory* (New York: Continuum, 1982), pp. 132–187.

26. Walter Buckley, *Sociology and Modern Systems Theory* (Englewood Cliffs, N.J.: Prentice-Hall, 1967), pp. 47, 58.

27. Parsons, *Societies: Evolutionary and Comparative Perspectives*, pp. 28–29.

28. Kenneth E. Boulding, "General Systems Theory—The Skeleton of Science," *Management Science 2* (April 1956): 197–208; Stafford Beer, *Cybernetics and Management* (New York: Wiley, 1959); Donald C. Malcolm, Alan J. Rowe, and Lorimer F. McConnell, *Management and Control Systems* (New York: Wiley, 1960).

29. Jacques Ellul, *The Technological Society*, trans. John Wilkinson (New York: Random House, 1964), pp. 80ff.

30. Martin Heidegger, "The Question concerning Technology," in Heidegger, *The Question concerning Technology and Other Essays*, trans. William Lovitt (New York: Harper and Row, 1977), pp. 3–35.

31. Edmund Husserl, *The Crisis of European Sciences and Transcendental Phenomenology*, trans. David Carr (Evanston, Ill.: Northwestern University Press, 1970), pp. 21–60.

32. Edward G. Ballard, "Man or Technology: Which Is to Rule," in Stephen Skousgaard, ed., *Phenomenology and the Understanding of Human Destiny* (Washington, D.C.: University Press of America, 1981), pp. 3–19.

33. This point is developed more extensively in the concluding chapter of this collection.

3

Automation and the Transformation of Work: Brooklyn Longshoremen as Reluctant Theorists and Practical Marxists

William DiFazio

This chapter describes the changes that occur in the daily life of workers as a result of technological changes at the workplace. Specifically, the effects of containerization on longshoremen is analyzed. This work is part of a study that explored how Brooklyn longshoremen on the Guaranteed Annual Income (GAI) maintain a working-class community.

The GAI enables longshoremen with high seniority, who have been displaced from full-time work because of automation, to work rarely and yet receive a full annual salary. The GAI has been in effect since 1966. Originally, it guaranteed all longshoremen the pay equivalent to 1,600 hours of work per year. In 1968, that was raised to the present level of 2,080 hours. Thus, as of 1984, all longshoremen have a guaranteed annual income of $32,000.

A key premise of this study is that these men have kept up earlier working-class cultural and political forms even though their work and nonwork situations have been altered by the GAI.[1] The informal level of dissent and resistance assumes the form of a social and cultural base of political action even when there is no formal or institutionalized political struggle or movement present.

LONGSHOREMEN AGAINST THE GAI

Typically, the majority of the men on the GAI claim that it is the best thing that ever happened to them. Other men on the GAI disagree. They take advantage of its benefits, yet they still have reservations about the GAI. These reservations are expressed in the following statements by Whitey★ and Babalu. Whitey states:

★These interviews were conducted with Brooklyn longshoremen from 1976–1980. This study was funded, in part, by a grant from the U.S. Department of Labor, Manpower Administration, 1978–1979.

The GAI ruined the manpower on the waterfront. You see years ago a man took a lot of pride in his work. He made sure that he produced.... Today I'd say they're happy in a way, but they're just getting paid for doing nothing. Years ago they'd go out and work; like now they won't go to work. They don't take no pride . . . it took pride away from a lot of men.

Babalu works three days a week and is on the GAI for the other two. Babalu states:

The guys are losing their work skills.... You wonder how much the deckman up on a winch retains after not working for so many years. The holdman—how much can he retain? How much can he stand on his back? Is he going up and down the ladder right? They're really out of shape. How can they work anymore when they have to? . . . Can they still do what has to be done? . . . [Before] working was talking, was sharing. It was eight hours of enrichment. There was satisfaction in storing the cargo the right way or talking about good or bad weather . . . that this happened or that happened. Now there is less to share among the workers.

Implicit in Babalu and Whitey's statements is their belief that the GAI has been beneficial for the shipping companies but not the men. The point of the GAI is to reduce manpower through a peaceful means. Thus, the GAI is a result of a conflict between work and automation.

Informally, workers have resisted the dissolution of the work-place through their recreation, solidarity in the hiring hall and their use of nonwork time. Accordingly, the transformation of the former cornerstone of the workplace—the old work gang—will be examined. The following discussion will assess four facets of the GAI criticized by Whitey and Babalu:

1. The GAI undermines the work skill and pride of work that was once part of the job.

2. The GAI ends the comradeship among workers on the piers.

3. Men on the GAI have "too much time on their hands" yet have failed to find meaningful ways to utilize their nonwork time.

4. The GAI has undermined the work ethic and thus reduced the productivity of workers.[2]

THE MEN'S EXPERIENCE OF WORK

According to the longshoremen, the introduction of capital-intensive technologies by shipping and stevedore companies dissolved the workplace community. Most important, as the men suggest, these technologies mostly benefit the shipping companies.

Lippy expresses a sense of loss about work that no longer requires skill. In the old days, "he rigged the winches by hand" but today this is no longer necessary, for "now everything is electrical." For Lippy, the breakup of the old work gang is related to the increasing mechanization of work.

I was seventeen when I started down on the waterfront. I hadn't graduated from high school. I started to shape up and started to work. After a while I got assigned to a gang. I started working on the dock. Manual labor. Everything had to be done by hand; it wasn't like now. There was actually a lot of lifting involved and we lifted everything. You had to be pretty strong physically. There were very few machines; everything was manual labor at the time.

It's all mechanical [now]. The older conventional ships all have electrical [equipment]. It's very easy to operate the newer equipment; you don't need any skill. It's interesting. It would be interesting; it's interesting to work the electrical machines. It takes less skill, definitely.

Bill also talks about becoming a longshoreman. In his account, the men worked in a shared, meaningful community, where the ties of friendship and family were primary. These ties continue to be the basis for community life among these men. His statement also illustrates the men's belief in a "work ethic" and their dedication to their work.

The deckmen at that time used to start at 7:00 in the morning; the gangs used to start at 8:00. My father was in and they shaped the men. And he'd call Tony's gang and the hold men and the dock gang, and I'd walk in with the dock gang. And I had no working clothes and I was dressed with two tone shoes on, plaid pants. So this Irish stevedore was looking at me and he yells, "Who's that kid." So my uncle says, "That's John's kid." Well he says, "If he's going to work you'd better get him some working clothes, because he can't work here tomorrow looking like that. Tell him to get a pair of overalls, a cap, and a pair of working shoes." So my uncle says, "Hear what he said." My uncle threw a bunch of slings down there [alongside the boat]. He said, "O.K., give me a draft." I didn't even know what a draft was. I asked my cousin. He said, "Don't ya worry; you come with me. I'll show you what to do." I started working with him and we made a draft—a draft is cargo; cases of cargo with a sling underneath. . . . And that was blood money. . . .

Oh boy, it isn't like that today. Now everything is palletized. I'm from the old school; see what they have today. These fellows come in with their dancing shoes and a wristwatch on their hands, and diamonds on their pinkies. Today they call for a break—they need this and they need that. . . . The hold job by no means is as difficult as it used to be. Now everything is strapped up; they even have bags strapped up. Coffee bags are strapped; rubber is strapped. It makes a difference. They produce more and the work is easier.

In Sabu's account, the importance of having a good partner is apparent. In any work gang, the men must depend on each other if the work is to be done efficiently without anyone getting hurt.

Right after the second war, I worked down the hold. I worked bags, nothing but bags—cement and flour bags. That's hard work. A flour bag is two hundred pounds—you'd lift them up and stack them with your partner. That's why you had to have a good partner. This is where teamwork came in. The two men had to depend on one another, otherwise you'd have your back broken. It was all manual labor. And you felt good at the end of the day.

Bill's account illustrates how men within the work gangs could facilitate change at the informal level. Racial integration of the higher categories required a formal union mandate, but that was not the whole story. Integration, as these workers suggest, could be initiated by the men to meet their needs. Bill integrated his gang because he wanted to have the best deckman.

My gang was the best gang. We were the best because we had the best deckmen. We had Lippy and Freddy. They were the best in all of Brooklyn. If you want to get the job done safely and quickly, you have to have good deckmen. When Freddy retired, I wanted the best winchman. I wanted someone as good as Freddy or Lippy. Sure I had blacks in the hold and on the pier, but no winchmen. So I asked Hank if he wanted to be my winchman. He said sure. A lot of men on other gangs said that I couldn't do this, that I couldn't have a black winchman. I told them I wanted the best, and Hank was the best. All I cared about was having the two best deckmen in Brooklyn—in getting the job done, with having the highest productivity, without getting anyone hurt.

The following two accounts by Tom and Babalu illustrate the men's understanding of how automation occurred on the waterfront and how it transformed their lives. Tom states:

No, I never thought it would be like this. I mean, I don't think the shipping companies knew themselves that it was going to come this fast. I mean we went from the small container, maybe a ten-foot container, to a forty-foot container. Now you got these LASH ships—a whole barge, 150 ton, they put the whole thing inside the ship. They pick it right out of the water and put it right on the ship.

Babalu says:

There was a class of ship [in 1951] that was loading that was called a notch ship. One of [its] features was that it had a concrete bottom. The inside of the ship was floored off with concrete, so that the high-lows could operate in the bottom of the hatch. So, what they were doing was taking the pallets and stacking them on top of another. They were using the high-low in the hatch. I had never seen that on the East Coast until I started working when . . . I was longshoring and I saw it happening . . . it was 1955 . . . 1956 . . . when they started putting the high-low in the hatch. It was apparent to me that they were really starting to move cargo in a faster way.

But as far as it . . . or what you could say was the genesis of it [automation] was small containers that were eight by eight, or could have been eight by ten. In other words, they were eight feet wide, eight feet high, and eight feet or ten feet long. . . .

So actually I think the use of the high-low in the hatch and the small containers, that were first introduced in the fifties, and then ya know the introduction of the new type of ship. First the ships came in with a great many containers, with conventional type booms, and it was very difficult to unload those containers. The introduction of more and more containers finally . . . the more feasible for the ships to be designed . . . exclusively for containers. . . . This is sort of the beginning of the container ship. The beginning of the type of ship that was gradually designed.

Then it started—the development of a versatile container itself. The original ones were all enclosed. They had new types of containers where the top of the container was opened, so that you could put different types of machinery in it. Eventually this led to the introduction of the LASH ship, which is the loading of complete barges through the after end of the ship. And in these barges they can hold, I think, four or five containers. So that eventually the outcome is going to be that there'll be no long-shoremen at all involved in different operations. . . . They [the companies] hire a gang for a whole ship . . . but I don't know what the hold men do on this ship. The winchmen don't do anything but, maybe, give a signal or something. Some places use half a gang on these LASH ships; some places use a full gang. But, in reality, when you talk about automation's impact on the waterfront, the ultimate goal of the shipowners is to eliminate the longshoremen altogether.

SUMMARY OF THE MEN'S ACCOUNTS OF THEIR WORK EXPERIENCE

The work was hard and physical strength was required. Few machines were used and almost all of the cargo was handled directly, often in terrible weather conditions. Often, the men would not find work even though they would spend a whole day shaping up at various piers. But the traditional structure of the work gang did give meaning to work.

The shipping companies developed capital-intensive technologies to increase their profits and stabilize the nature of work on the docks. This resulted in work that was not demanding physically. Technology also displaced thousands of workers and led to the degradation of their skills.[3] As a result, workers with less skill were required.

Yet it is the dissolution of the work gang that explains the men's informal resistance to work. Outside of the traditional gang, labor is no longer meaningful, because the traditional social bonds that govern work no longer exist. Men are now assigned to a gang in the hiring hall. Thus, they are no longer part of the primary group relations of the old work community. In the process of shaping up in the hiring hall, they work in a gang as strangers. As Sabu said, "You are low man on the totem pole."

The men in the hiring hall are not resisting work in general but work that is no longer meaningful. If the community could be reconstituted, as Sabu says, "They'd go back to work tomorrow."

Since the community is not likely to be reconstituted because of the shipping companies' commitment to capital-intensive technologies, workers create their community elsewhere, for example, in the hiring hall and during their nonwork time.

THEORETICAL IMPLICATIONS OF AUTOMATION

When a job is physically difficult and dangerous, workers must cooperate with each other. Without the partnership system, it would be impossible, for example, to stack 200-pound bags of flour four high. The cooperative nature of work led the men to value each other. In Bill's account, being a good worker is more important than a worker's racial identity. According to the values of the waterfront gang, the highest praise one worker can give another is to call him a "working stiff." The sharing of labor meant that they all shared the burden of work, including the culture of the workplace.

Although it is greatly transformed, this community still exists in the hiring hall or, in other words, at the informal level. This explains how men separated and degraded by automation still maintain their political position in the ongoing struggle between the shipping companies and the union.

It is at the informal level that the resistance and accommodation that are part of all political struggles appear. The men are not only involved in informal resistance to work but, additionally, are beginning to understand these actions in a critical way. This process of developing a critical understanding of work transforms them into what might be called reluctant theorists and practical Marxists. These men display a practical sense of Karl Marx's labor theory when they answer the charges that they receive pay without working. Furthermore, they believe that they won the GAI through a union struggle and years of hard work on the piers of New York.[4]

They theorize that they have produced profits for the shipping and stevedore companies that far exceed the wages that they have been paid. Sabu, for example, displays this practical Marxism when he states: "They've made more profits than you could possibly think of. Has to be, and I and many people in my category made them the profits over the years."

Sabu and most other longshoremen do not see themselves as

Marxists or social theorists. However, their work experiences have enabled them to develop a version of the labor theory of value and exploitation. They understand that they have been paid less than their worth, and, furthermore, that without their labor there would be no profits. This is clear from Big Tom's statement:

> They [the companies] say they want to do more stripping and stuffing [loading and unloading containers on the piers]. On the other hand, the shipping companies don't want the stripping and stuffing done by long-shoremen because it's too expensive.
>
> All they really care about is reducing costs. And they'll try and do it any way they can. . . .
>
> Ten million manhours. Where do you think they get that much money to pay us that much GAI? Surplus profits. It all comes out of surplus profits. Who do you think made their profits? Who do you think?

To reiterate, the men are in no sense formal Marxists. For these men, Marxism means Stalinism and totalitarianism. Yet their theorizing about the origin of profit is true to the spirit of Marx's critique of capitalism, for clearly they view their collective labor as producing value that they do not share. For Marx, the labor theory of value is the social form that value production takes in capitalist society.[5]

The labor theory of value links socially human productive activity, or work, to the marketplace where commodities are exchanged, and thus workers are related directly to the world of capital and capitalists. Marx's theory of value is not only an economic theory but a social theory. For it is social production by workers that creates value and, thus, surplus value. Marx explains this process as follows:

> Capitalist production is not merely the production of commodities, it is essentially the production of surplus-value. The laborer produces, not for himself but for capital. It no longer suffices, therefore, that he should simply produce. He must produce surplus-value. That laborer alone is productive, who produces surplus-value for the capitalist, and thus works for the self-expansion of capital. If we may take an example from outside the sphere of production of material objects, a schoolmaster is a productive laborer when in addition to belaboring the heads of his scholars, he works like a horse to enrich the school proprietor. That the latter has laid out his

capital in a teaching factory, instead of a sausage factory does not alter the relation. Hence the notion of productive labor implies not only a relation between work and useful effect, between laborer and the product of labor, but also a specific social relation of production, a relation that has sprung up historically and stamps the laborer as the direct means of creating surplus-value.[6]

In the same way that Sabu and Big Tom have theorized as practical Marxists, so does Bowly:

Well, eventually they are going to get rid of us; there's a lot less of us now, you know.

They're making more [money] now than years ago. They [the companies] quadrupled their profits because of containerization. It used to take us ten to twelve days to unload a ship. Now a ship comes in and they discharge it and load it in twenty-four hours . . . it's out of port again. This makes up a lot of time.

Look at the ships that are coming in. They have ships that carry 200 containers. Do you realize how much cargo that is and it can be loaded and unloaded in a day? Do you know how much money that is? They're making hundreds of millions of dollars. The GAI is like a drop in the bucket for them, and the newspapers make such a stink about it. The shippers make millions, the stevedores make millions, and the companies that make containers make millions. How much profit would they make without us? We worked like animals all these years. We made millions for them and they [newspapers] make a stink about it. What do they know?

As practical Marxists, longshoremen on the GAI are not theorists or revolutionaries. What they illustrate is that they have common-sense notions of exploitation and surplus value. It is in these terms that they understand the GAI as earned. As Bowly said, "It's getting even." The GAI represents "getting even" with the class of shipowners and stevedores who have profited from the labor of the longshoremen. As practical Marxists, the longshoremen understand the GAI to be the focal point of a class struggle, and the GAI signals a partial victory for them.

This victory over the shipowners and stevedores reinforces their sense of community. The men not only have a similar work experience, but also have struggled together for the GAI. Through this struggle, the men on the GAI have won back a portion of the profits they originally produced.

This section concludes with a militant statement by Baldo, a carpenter. His words clearly illustrate how the men are practical Marxists:

> Neighbors ask me if I'm working, or "why I'm home so early." I tell them I worked nights or late afternoons. It's none of their fucking business. If I told them they'd make a big thing about it. How unfair it is; how easy I have it; how lazy I am. I say fuck them. They didn't give a shit about me when I was working my balls off. About that they didn't care; they never said it was unfair when we worked day and night for seven days a week—that was all right. Let them all fuck themselves.
>
> They don't know. I would call my brother and we would shape up on Sunday afternoons; sometimes we wouldn't get work and sometimes we would work to twelve at night, and then be at the hall at 6:30 Monday morning. Those fucks don't know what hard work is. We've earned this [GAI].

In their understanding of the world, the senior longshoremen clearly ground the present in a workplace community that is based in the past of the old work gang.

BEYOND WORK

In summary, this chapter describes how senior Brooklyn long-shoremen have struggled informally against the shipping compa-nies' introduction of automation. Their struggle assumes the form of opting for pay without work. In effect, as practical Marxists, their battle cry is "no work without community."

Thousands of longshoremen have been displaced by container cranes and containerized cargo. The GAI can be viewed as a con-servative solution to technological domination because it allows for the development of a workerless place that minimizes costs and maximizes productivity. However, the men perceive the GAI as a form of resistance. As practical Marxists, they demand that shipping companies pay the human costs of automation. These men are "getting even"; they are getting back a portion of the "surplus profits" they created. These longshoremen, who have worked hard all of their lives, have attached themselves to a nonproductivist ideology in which their well-being and freedom are promoted through their refusal to be productive. As reluctant theorists, they view productivity as opposed to their interests and beneficial to the shipping companies, as it represents increased output without an accompanying increase in wages. In a sense, they have recaptured part of their lives because their time is now their own.

NOTES

1. Edward Palmer Thompson, *The Making of the English Working Class* (New York: Vintage Books, 1963).

2. Gene Ruffini, "The 70G a Year Dock Worker," *New York Post*, February 1, 1979, p. 6. Joseph Martin and Brian Kates, "500 Longshoremen Got 20G for No Work in '78," *Daily News*, February 2, 1970, p. 17.

3. Harry Braverman, *Labor and Monopoly Capital* (New York: Monthly Review Press, 1974).

4. Ruffini, "The 70G a Year Dock Worker," p. 6.

5. I. I. Rubin, *Essays on Marx's Theory of Value* (Detroit: Black and Red, 1972), p. 69.

6. Karl Marx, *Capital*, vol. 1 (New York: International Publishers, 1968), p. 509.

4

Technology, Humanism, and Death by Injection: Strange Bedfellows?

John W. Murphy

A new spectre has emerged on the American scene, yet its overall social implications remain mostly unexplored. Recent events in Texas have illustrated that it is possible to refine the act of killing by making this practice highly technological. The popular press has referred to this process as an attempt to humanize executions by replacing the executioner's block with high-tech instruments.[1] Nevertheless, the idea that humanism and killing can be intimately associated is quite paradoxical. What kind of legerdemain is present when the public can be convinced that there is anything humane about taking the life of a human being? How has it come to be the case that technological killing is considered to be more humane than any other form, or that killing can contribute to enhancing the human condition? As Herbert Marcuse suggests, the appearance of this style of contradictory thinking is indicative of serious social problems that may escalate to the point that all order is jeopardized.[2]

In order to understand how killing made technological can be appraised as humane, a brief review of a few crucial philosophical gambits must be undertaken. First, the impact of Cartesianism on thinking in general must be assessed. Second, the key characteristics of modern technology must be specified so that the tableau of social life that they outline is rendered apparent. And third, the image of human existence advanced by technology must be illustrated while emphasizing how technology, humanism, and killing can be interrelated without much consternation. Throughout this presentation, the work of Michel Foucault on punishment and rehabilitation will be regularly consulted because he has addressed this issue and laid the necessary foundation for criticizing the use of technology as a "humanistic" mode of execution.

As Foucault points out in his book *Discipline and Punish*, the history of punishment can be characterized as a perennial search for a more humane way of inflicting public censure.[3] Yet the question remains, what is meant by the term humane? If the reader looks closely, it is discovered that the usual ways of conceptualizing humanism are not followed. For example, humane treatment is not associated with a concern for the quality of social life, an appreciation of the uniqueness of the person, enhancing human potential, or judicial fairness. Instead, humane treatment simply does not offend human sensibilities, and therefore cannot be graphic, spectacular, or terroristic. A humane form of punishment is refined, precise, and, put frankly, conceals its violent nature. Foucault suggests that this is achieved by punishment assuming an increasingly abstract form, divorced from the interpersonal reality that finds its violent character repugnant.

Nevertheless, how is it possible for abstractness to obscure the tempestuous side of punishment? What type of philosophy is capable of successfully deanimating particular violent acts so that they do not appear to be humanly motivated? If interpersonal violence is unacceptable, how is it possible for technology to impose suffering in a dispassionate manner? How can reason be associated with abstract technological acts, while nonreason is considered to be inherent to any act that questions the legitimacy of these rarefied procedures?

In order to answer these queries, the theoretical demarche inaugurated by René Descartes (circa 1600) must be understood. As a matter of fact, Foucault declares that a significant shift in thinking took place at that time that changed the manner in which punishment was conceived. The change that Foucault is referring to is the acceptance of what is nowadays called Cartesian dualism. This philosophical method represents a variant of the enlightenment tradition that hoped to supply knowledge with an apodictic base as opposed to the purely speculative ground promulgated by the Church fathers during the medieval period. In order to accomplish this, however, reliable knowledge could not be associated with the capriciousness thought to be indigenous to human acts, which formerly offered only apologies for the theology of Rome. Rather, knowledge and human cognition would have to be irrevocably distinguished so that unbiased or pristine knowledge might be discovered. As Foucault describes this maneuver, the passion of human existence is categorically removed from the realm of reason.[4] Human eroticism is replaced by a science of the body, thereby establishing an abstract frame of reference for corporal punishment. Thus, objective measures that are divorced categorically from human sentiments serve to specify the parameters of reasonable action.

As should be immediately noted, Cartesianism has immense social consequences. Of key importance is the idea that certain forms of knowledge are treated as if they are not connected to the human element of social existence. This separation of fact from value is certainly an illusion because a disembodied phenomenon would be as ineffable as Immanuel Kant's "*Ding-an-sich.*" In other words, knowledge without perception is very difficult to justify. Nonetheless, according to Cartesianism, impassioned acts are classified differently from those that originate from reason. Because acts of reason are presumed to be objective, they are also thought to be fair, just, and suitable for universal consumption. Stated simply, the rules of reason reflect standards of demeanor that are assumed to be acceptable to every rational person simply because they are unrelated to the contingency or idiosyncrasy of individually motivated actions.

This type of thinking obviously places a serious strain on the strategies that are used by people to organize their everyday lives. Particularly, the language, symbols, and customs that are employed to regulate the social world and ensure its continuity cannot be understood to be objective, for they convey the history of their creators. The modalities of cognition that are considered to be indicative of reason must, nevertheless, deny their historicity, as Friedrich Nietzsche says. To use Weberian phraseology, reason must purge itself of all contact with the substantive or human dimension of existence so that the supposedly universal nature of reason is not tainted by the corrupting influence of existential concern.[5] As Max Weber also points out, however, this provides reason with a false sense of autonomy. Nevertheless, it is precisely this type of ahistorical recognition that reason demands if it is to fulfill its role of providing objective or impartial guidelines for ordering social life.

Following Descartes, what has happened essentially is that human action is left to confront a world that it cannot influence. As Jean Gebser notes, the assumed objectivity of the world represents a rational will that can successfully constrain the passionate side of existence.[6] Reason supplies the "reality principle" that Sigmund Freud believed would harness the irrational dynamism that allegedly motivates human beings. Accordingly, the farther a phenomenon is removed from the affect of passion, the more rational it is thought to be. The less passionate an act is, the more humane it becomes because human beings are portrayed to be acting as "rational animals."[7] Once this personal status is attained, it is assumed that humanism can begin to flourish.

The general upshot of Cartesianism is that abstractness is equated with humanness. A primary index of humanness in the seventeenth century was the degree to which passion or capriccio was not witnessed in the procedures used to enact punishment. Subsequently, numerous attempts were made to remove the apparent human element from frequently used punitive and rehabilitative strategies by making them increasingly abstract, thus giving them the facade of being dispassionate. Foucault copiously documents how this was accomplished.

He argues that the field of medicine became ostensibly humane by following a couple of tactics that gave it an air of respectability. For instance, medicine ceased addressing the issue of health and instead concerned itself with guaranteeing normalcy.[8] In order to accomplish this, practitioners tried to mimic the laws of nature and treat the patient as an "object" of study[9] by thoroughly mathematizing and formalizing all medical procedures.[10] Similar to the gambit made much later by the members of the Vienna Circle, a "measured" language was adopted that was envisioned to be precise and scientific.[11] This, of course, was Latin. Eventually, medicine was able to project a favorable image of itself because logic seemed to be directing its development.

Eighteenth-century reformers followed a similar path in treating mental illness. It is commonly known that the treatment of mental illness has a checkered past, which includes demonology, alchemy, and a varied assortment of savage remedies, including outright torture. Foucault contends that faulty reasoning led to this state of affairs, as an inhumane *pathos* underpinned all diagnostic efforts.[12] As a corrective, psychiatry strove to become a positive science and adopt the methods of the physical sciences that were gaining public support at the time. Psychiatry, therefore, tried to enlist the highest ideals of reason when treating patients in order to avoid engaging in acts of vengeance similar to those of former practitioners who were scandalized by the manifestation of such a heinous form of nonreason as mental illness and attempted to suppress it at all cost. In other words, modern therapists developed a fully formalized and rigorous diagnostic nomenclature, including equally scientific and tested treatment options specifically designed for each malady. It was assumed that psychiatry would become increasingly humane with each successful attempt to make diagnosis and treatment more rational.[13]

The history of criminal punishment can be characterized similarly. Since the early work of Cesare Beccaria, the general trend has been to reduce the arbitrariness of the criminal justice system and thus render it more humane. The clearest example of this is present in Jeremy Bentham's work and the views of his modern followers, who are sometimes referred to as neo-utilitarians or deterrent theorists. As Foucault suggests, no longer was a criminal to experience the traditional "thousand deaths" inflicted by imprecise acts of torture, but instead an abstract calculus designed to dispense exact amounts of punishment appropriate for a particular crime was invented.[14] Subsequently, it was believed the excesses that usually accompanied punishment could be minimized. In order to ensure objectivity, however, the criminal justice system would have to institute what Foucault calls psychological "disconnectors," which would allow punishment to be perceived as indifferent to the nature of an offense or the identity of a malefactor.

The notion of "generalized punishment" eventually surfaced in the form of an "autonomous" legal system that was thought to provide equal justice for all persons, simply because it appeared to be unrelated to personal or class interests.[15] All the "biographical" elements of crime were to be extirpated from the judicial process so that court dispositions could not be swayed by the nonreason indigenous to the corporeal side of life.[16] Law, as Weber says, was no longer thought to have a conventional nature simply because the violation of this type of grounded order typically provokes a violent and severe response from a community. Normalcy, instead, became scientific, with justice and humanity the result of "meticulous calculation."[17] The aim of this trend was to establish an economy of crime and punishment on an abstract formula of justice.

Of key importance is the idea that a person or society becomes humane by the exercise of reason. This type of reason, however, represents a break with the pernicious or furtive nature of an embodied existence. In fact, madness represents the interjection of the body into the pure light of reason, thus creating a penumbra that shelters the dark forces of life. A personal or social existence that is grounded on reason must operate according to an abstract or cosmological law that is untainted by the shadow cast by the body. As Nietzsche declares, a human existence necessarily bloodies itself through contact with the world, yet it is precisely this kind of contamination that reason scorns. Reason must be pure, chaste, and unadulterated by the contingency of corporeally motivated acts. Until this state of reason is achieved justice will remain suspect, which suggests that justice must constantly spurn the body.

For many modern theorists, the bane of technology is that it conveys the countenance of a socially disembodied existence, a life disconnected from the flesh. For instance, Marcuse envisions technology to be a "veil" that masks all social relationships.[18] Both Niklas Luhmann[19] and Maurice Merleau-Ponty[20] say it removes the ambiguity from history and basically unburdens the individual from having to make vital decisions pertaining to the direction life will take. This happens, according to Ludwig Landgrebe[21] and Don Ihde[22], because technology is thoroughly abstract and appears to receive its directives from an ahistorical *eschaton* that deanimates everyday life by eviscerating human *praxis* (action). It is for these reasons that technology is considered by many to represent the highest development of reason or the clearest manifestation of unadulterated thinking that is immaculately conceived.

Jacques Ellul describes succinctly what is believed to be the strength of technological thinking: It has eclipsed its human origin and through its glistening, pristine features actively denies that it has a corporeal existence. As a result, technology emanates from the pure light of reason and liberates itself from mere bodily concerns. Of sole importance for technology is the refinement of precision, economy, and increased efficiency. Technology does not appear to be a part of life, thus possessing a visceral dimension, but is able to transcend all bodily limitations and soar above life and correct its foibles. As Ellul says, "technology has become autonomous."[23] He contends that it is no longer a tool to be used, but is currently accorded the metaphysical status formerly reserved for gods. As such, technology provides its own abstract answers to equally rarefied problems. Presumably, it is precisely this rationale that is used to justify technology as a humane method of killing because the only problems associated with this act are thought to be technological.

It seems as if we have come a full circle in our thinking. Reason becomes nonreason since the former denies any contact with human concerns and issues, yet is is just this state of affairs the advocates of reason find desirable. Technology begins to think while this human ability begins to atrophy, and thus social issues are assessed solely in terms of what is considered to be technically problematic. Yet, as Martin Heidegger continually reminds his readers, technology does not really think and does nothing on its own. Nonetheless, because of its abstract nature, technology obscures ethical and social issues by portraying them as technologically unimportant. As Foucault points out, nonutilitarian questions are viewed by technological rationality as useless and representative of madness or "sin."[24] It is these corporeal questions of existence, however, that philosophers throughout the ages believed prompted people to improve the human condition. The question that remains is: Does technological reason offer an ideal for judging human actions, or does it obscure the human condition altogether and avoid the tough issues that must be addressed if the quality of social life is to improve? In order to properly answer this question, some of the possible repercussions of technological killing must be explored.

First, as writers like Marcuse and Jurgen Habermas contend, this move to technological killing obfuscates the social and political issues associated with capital punishment. Foucault suggests that this was one of the intended goals of those who originally pushed for the increased rationalization of discipline.[25] No longer should punishment be portrayed as a confrontation between the sovereign state and the condemned person, which tends to arouse the ire of the public. Any relationship that punishment might have to political power, social control, or social issues in general can be obscured if a penalty is thoroughly rationalized and given the appearance of emanating from natural law. Punishment, therefore, would not be perceived as idiosyncratic, but can be touted as reflecting the "general will" that supposedly underpins a social policy. Of course, when a society is in a period of crisis, as is the American society today, this method of dealing with a social problem such as crime becomes very appealing.

Nevertheless, this supposedly neutral approach to addressing crime may eventually backfire on those who try to use it. Specifically, no politician really wants to be closely linked to policies that are obscene or atrocious, and therefore political alliances are somewhat downplayed by those who advocated capital punishment in the past. As a result of recent technological advancements, however, supporting the idea of state executions may not appear to be politically risky and, subsequently, particular political parties may begin to align themselves openly with this anticrime strategy. If particular parties can be directly related to this political solution to crime, instead of implying that it represents the moral will of the public (a general axiom), the true ideological nature of crime policy can be revealed. To the chagrin of those who want to gloss over the social and political implications of crime, anticrime policies may become thoroughly politicized. Reason, accordingly, tries to subsume political conflicts only to have them manifested in another form.

Second, technology as reason eschews all discussion about the ethical character of punishment. In point of fact, reason finds ethical questions to be extremely disruptive. Technological solutions to crime are merely concerned with ensuring that all procedures are logical, clearly operationalized, consistent, and precise. Whether they are fair is of no concern to technology. However, as the theorists associated with the so-called Brussels Circle suggest, laws must not merely be rational for them to retain their social support, but also must be fair.[26] The issue of fairness, moreover, is thoroughly political because it pertains to public perception of law and order. If law enforcement is not sensitive to a community's sense of justice, social injustice occurs. Nothing will rapidly mobilize a community faster than the belief that its members are being treated unfairly.

Again, this is exactly the opposite effect desired by those who want to rationalize the judicial process. Although at first the use of technology may appear to be politically neutral, this lack of concern for the issue of fairness may generate political upheaval. When technology was not used to execute criminals, discussions of fairness were prevalent, which may have served the ignoble function of a political palliative. Nevertheless, the decline in ethical discussions resulting from the increased use of technology may serve to illustrate the brutal nature of capital punishment and demonstrate the need for a political solution to the problem of crime.[27] Even though reason is commonly thought to be fair, its failure to confront the issue of social fairness directly may again inadvertently transform reason into nonreason.

Third, those who believe that capital punishment prevents crime view technology to be the most appropriate method for properly operationalizing the utilitarian viewpoint on which deterrent philosophy is based. Technology may in fact facilitate the institution of E. Van den Haag's ideal judicial system, where laws are enforced in a truly calculated manner so that they resemble an intractable "threat system" from which criminals cannot escape without receiving their just deserts.[28]

However, because of the abstract nature of technology, it may not serve as a deterrent to crime. How can the pain inflicted by technology be envisioned by the potential criminal? Technology is by design noncorporeal as it barely touches the body, and the killing that results is "silent." Because the social nature of an execution is intentionally concealed, the social repercussions of a crime also may be obscured. All the potential criminal may have is a vague notion of a technological sentence that has no social significance. As John Stuart Mill more than adequately pointed out, Bentham's "calculus of felicity" has a social side that the latter ignored. It is for this reason the younger Mill felt Bentham's proposed penal system would never work, since he underestimated seriously the "human quotient" present in any pain-happiness ratio. Since technology eliminates totally this human element of punishment, it may create an esoteric conception of pain that cannot be appreciated or evaluated. Accordingly, the social cost of crime may be reduced instead of increased because criminal behavior has no bodily referent.

And fourth, technology conveys a scientific image of the social world, as if society were a machine, system, or some other inert object. Modern theorists, such as those associated with the critical school and *praxis* group, maintain that this view of society is an unmitigated ideology. What they mean by this is that the social world is portrayed as an abstract set of roles and tasks that must be performed for a social system to survive. Laws, accordingly, merely reflect the structure of the system and not concrete interpersonal relationships. As Foucault suggests, technology masks the social interaction that underpins law, and thus crime is no longer thought to be implicated in a matrix of social relations.[29] Subsequently, the social factors that delimit criminal behavior are considered to be unimportant, and crime prevention becomes a technological problem of preserving the social system.

Yet it cannot be forgotten that crime is fundamentally a social issue. Even utilitarian theories presuppose this when terms like guilt, social good, and injury are used. Crime is thoroughly a corporeal act that can only be addressed in bodily and not technological terms. Because technology eliminates the body, victims of crime are not real to criminals, economic conditions are not interpersonal but systemic, courts are not violent, and the social world is not flesh but something to be attacked in a calculated manner. Without the body, criminal justice is a farce, for its deals with abstractions that overlook issues such as fairness or justice. Due to the fact that technology depicts abstractly the social world, criminal behavior may be promoted because the adverse effects crime has on the social body are unknown. Crime, therefore, is based on pure calculation that ignores human life, for the criminal is disembodied and cannot understand the human sentiment that is central to both deterrence and punishment. Criminals are then merely machines that neither live nor die.

Only when the human side of crime is addressed can justice be approached rationally, as opposed to stressing merely technological solutions to criminal behavior. This is what the classical social philosophers tried to teach their students. Yet because the social issues that must be addressed for existence to improve are ignored by technology, the quality of life may appear momentarily to be improving while it is actually deteriorating and becoming increasingly barbaric. Technology, in a sense, may be blinding persons to the extent that their personal needs and environment are subordinated to technique, thereby eliminating questions that pertain to their social responsibility. Eventually, however, the technological society must resurrect the existential questions that are basic to life or else diminish human existence altogether.

NOTES

1. Kurt Anderson, "An Eye for an Eye," *Time* 121, no. 4 (January 24, 1983): 28–39.

2. Herbert Marcuse, *One-Dimensional Man* (Boston: Beacon Press, 1964), pp. 88ff.

3. Michel Foucault, *Discipline and Punish*, trans. Alan Sheridan (New York: Pantheon Books, 1977).

4. Michel Foucault, *Madness and Civilization*, trans. Richard Howard (New York: Pantheon Books, 1965, p. 86.

5. Max Weber, *Social and Economic Organizations*, trans. A. M. Henderson and Talcott Parsons (New York: Free Press, 1947), pp. 35ff.

6. John W. Murphy, "Jean Gebser: A Guide for Humanistic Rhetorical Analysis," *Reflections* 2 (Winter 1981): 70–84.

7. Foucault, *Madness and Civilization*, p. 78.

8. Michel Foucault, *The Birth of the Clinic*, trans. A.M. Sheridan Smith (New York: Vintage Books, 1975), p. 35.

9. Ibid., p. 86.

10. Ibid., p. 104.

11. Ibid., pp. 114–115.

12. Michel Foucault, *Mental Illness and Psychology*, trans. Alan Sheridan (New York: Harper and Row, 1976), p. 64.

13. David Ingleby, "Understanding 'Mental Illness,' " in David Ingleby, ed., *Critical Psychiatry* (New York: Pantheon Books, 1980), pp. 23–71.

14. Foucault, *Discipline and Punish*, p. 12.

15. Ibid., p. 232.

16. Ibid., p. 252.

17. Ibid., p. 92.

18. Marcuse, *One-Dimensional Man*, p. 32.

19. Niklas Luhmann, *The Differentiation of Society*, trans. Stephen Holmes and Charles Larmore (New York: Columbia University Press, 1982), p. 317.

20. Svetozar Stojanović, *In Search of Democracy in Socialism* (Buffalo, N.Y.: Prometheus Books, 1981), pp. 110–120.

21. Ludwig Landgrebe, *Kritik and Metaphysic* (Berlin: de Gruyter, 1966), p. 228.

22. Don Ihde, "The Historical-Ontological Priority of Technology over Science," paper presented at the International Conference on Philosophy and Science in Phenomenological Perspective, Buffalo, N.Y., March 1982.

23. Jacques Ellul, *The Technological Society* (New York: Random House, 1964), p. 6.

24. Foucault, *Madness and Civilization*, p. 58.

25. Foucault, *Discipline and Punish*, pp. 73–103.

26. Chaim Perelman and L. Olbrechts-Tyteca, *The New Rhetoric: A Treatise on Argumentation*, trans. John Wilkinson and Purcell Weaver (Notre Dame, Ind.: University of Notre Dame Press, 1968).

27. William J. Bowers and Glenn L. Pierce, "Deterrence or Brutalization: What Is the Effect of Executions," *Crime and Delinquency* 26 (4) (October 1980): 453–484.

28. E. Van den Haag, "The Criminal Law as a Threat System," *The Journal of Criminal Law and Criminology* 73 (2) (1982): 769–785.

29. Foucault, *Mental Illness and Psychology*, pp. 82ff.

5

The Role of Reason in the Social Control of Mental Illness

Lisa A. Callahan and Dennis R. Longmire

FROM MADNESS TO MENTAL ILLNESS

Throughout history, societies have identified some people as being "mad." This chapter discusses the historical development of the concept of "madness," social reactions to those who are identified as mad, and implications of the medical approach to madness.

Early Societies

Greek, Roman, and Christian histories, as depicted in their works of art and literature, are replete with anecdotes and descriptions of those who were considered mad.[1] Yet these persons have not always been viewed as "mentally ill" or having a disease of the "mind" that requires official attention. From ancient times through the late Middle Ages, mentally deranged individuals were left in the community as long as they caused no major disturbance. Madness, in this sense, was a public issue.

In ancient societies (500 B.C. to A.D. 200), the mad were often seen as prophets. The trances, hallucinations, and voices experienced by them were regarded as visions of the future. During these early periods mentally deranged persons were left in the community; those who were wealthy hired a personal attendant, and a person who was dangerous was sometimes confined, restrained, or placed in the stocks. Yet the mad were regarded as socially incompetent and not necessarily legally or medically infirmed.[2] Communities identified and reacted negatively to those whose behaviors fell outside tolerable limits, nonetheless, this censure was based on social discourse and not rules thought to exist *sui generis*.

Greek and Roman mythology include stories of gods spreading

mental derangement as punishment.[3] During the early Greek and Roman periods, reactions to the mad combined fear, contempt, and a little compassion. Because the gods were the source of madness, the mad were simply avoided. By the fifth century B.C., beliefs about the causes of mental illness began to include medical explanations. Due to the emerging medical perspective, mentally deranged individuals were often the target of attack as supernatural "causes" began to be replaced by physiological explanations of madness. However, as with the ancient Hebrews and Romans, nonviolent madmen and madwomen were tolerated in the community, yet prohibited from making contracts, marrying, and acquiring or disposing of property. In both these periods identification and treatment of the mad were based upon social class. Those who were monied hired doctors to treat madness and attendants to protect the mad from harm. Stated simply, illness was still a social phenomenon.

Throughout the Middle Ages (sixth to thirteenth centuries) and the Renaissance (fourteenth to mid-seventeenth centuries) the mad also remained in their communities. Reactions to the mad paralleled those taken in ancient societies.[4] Social responses to the mad were ambiguous and based upon supernatural or metaphysical views of the individual and social reality. Yet madness was seen as part of an individual's total experiences. Reactions to the mad, therefore, were varied and included tolerance, banishment, and ridicule.[5] However, the absence of absolute reason allowed for illness to remain a social determination. With the onset of the classical era, attitudes toward madness changed. Explanations of madness and social reactions to the mad stressed individual weakness. Madness was a condition to be hidden from public view and repressed. Moreover, madness had to be controlled because it threatened public rationality. The houses of confinement built in the seventeenth century symbolized new social views of madness. Madness became equated with deviance. As Michel Foucault writes, "A sensibility was born which had drawn a line and laid a cornerstone, and which chose—only to banish."[6] For reason had to be restored through any means possible.

Modern Societies

It was not until what Foucault refers to as the "great confinement" in 1656 that physicians were given primary responsibility to care for the mind.[7] This had a profound effect on the public's reactions to the mad. Shortly after its opening in 1656, the Hospital General of Paris housed 6,000 persons, or one percent of that city's population.[8] The purpose for the confinement of thousands of persons was not for medical treatment, as only ten percent of the arrests for the Hospital General were for insanity.[9] According to Foucault, this mass confinement related to laws that prohibited begging and unemployment. Stated simply, idleness was condemned. During this time, work was equated with virtue, while idleness was considered immoral. The Protestant work ethic underpinned the administrative philosophy of the government's houses of confinement. Because of their inability to secure regular work, mad persons came to the attention of the police. When confined they were often unable to perform their chores, especially compared with their simply poor coinhabitants. Thus, the confined insane became doubly repressed and twice as immoral.

The confinement era was not humanistic, as often claimed. Proponents of confinement in both Europe and the United States frequently claimed that this was a humane response, a paternalistic reaction to the "less fortunate" members of society. Yet confinement was nihilistic. Its aim was to destroy madness and restore the individual to reason, or a rational state of mind. Absolute reason dominated both philosophy and public policy. The means for instilling "reason" were often painful, dehumanizing, and ineffective.[10] Nonetheless, restoring reason was the primary goal of confinement.

Unreasonable individuals became targets of scandal, hidden from public view, and denied liberty. They were treated like animals; the dangerous were chained to walls at their beds.[11] The mad became beasts. "For classicism, madness in its ultimate form is man in immediate relation to his animality, without reference, without any recourse."[12] Treatment for these "beasts" was discipline and brutality, all designed to render a person rational.

The Emergence of Mental Disease and Medical Treatment

Until the beginning of the seventeenth century, the four humours—blood, phlegm, and yellow and black bile—accounted for melancholia and mania. The qualities of each humour, coldness, hotness, dryness, and wetness, could alter the temperament of a person and cause madness. Hypochondria and hysteria were considered mental diseases late in the classical period. Medical explanations for these were not as simple as for melancholia and mania. Yet an evolution occurred from explaining mental illness in terms of the spreading of essences to locating illness in, for example, the nervous system. This shift in explanation was possible only because of increasing knowledge about human physiology. It was with these "diseases of the nerves" and "hysterias" that psychiatry was born.[13]

The therapies of the classical period can be grouped as follows: consolidation—the ingestion of substances, such as iron filings, which promote a reunion of body and soul; purification—the ingestion of corrosive substances, such as soap or scabies, to unclot the blood; immersion—water treatment, or hydrotherapy, which absolves the soul; and regulation—the control of movement by contraptions, such as the rotary machine,[14] to calm irritated nerves.[15]

In addition to these "treatments," the mad were "awakened" to their illness by making them feel guilty for being unable to cope with the stresses of daily life. Because of the regimentation and morality present in mental institutions, madness could not prevail. The organization and discipline within these institutions enabled reason to dominate madness. Most significant for modern psychiatry is the "reduction of the classical experience of unreason to a strictly moral perception of madness, which would secretly serve as a nucleus for all the concepts that the nineteenth century would subsequently vindicate as scientific, positive, and experimental."[16] Confinement as a rational "cure" for nonreason or mental illness became simply accepted and expected. Reason could be restored only if individuals took responsibility for their madness. Because of this belief in individual responsibility, mental illness became a personal problem, a step necessary for the medical model to prevail. Accordingly, no longer was society accountable for the mad.

The eighteenth-century insane were removed from the common houses of detention to the asylum, further separating them from society. Four characteristics are peculiar to the asylum experience: silence, recognition, perpetual judgment, and medical evaluations. The last factor is the most significant for modern psychiatry and the treatment of madness, as insanity and medicine became inextricably linked. By the end of the eighteenth century, a medical certificate was necessary for a person to be institutionalized. Treatment was not so much medical, but rather the asylum doctor was seen as a "wise man." The deranged were treated as children, incompetent yet, paradoxically, potentially responsible. Many of the treatments were actually punishments for patients who failed to adapt to the asylum. For example, the purification ritual of the shower was used to punish those who would not admit to being mad. The successful asylum maintained absolute order through the total domination of patients. Patients were watched closely and required to participate in rituals such as "tea parties." Awkwardness or errors in etiquette were regarded as failures and justification for further confinement. Thus, as Foucault explains, "The science of mental disease, as it would develop in the asylum, would always be only of the order of observation and classification."[17]

Despite investigations into the conditions in public and private institutions, which revealed abuses by medical personnel, the goal of review committees was not the removal of the medical staff. In fact, the absence of medical treatment was seen as neglect because of the commonly held belief that physical ailments always accompany mental disease.[18] Even in the absence of empirical support, physicians were successful in convincing the public that insanity was a medical problem, and reason would be restored only through the use of scientific, objective, and empirical medical protocol. By the mid-nineteenth century in Europe, lay reformers were content to allow doctors to maintain their seignorial position in mental institutions.

In the United States, reactions to the mad paralleled those in Europe. In colonial times, institutions were used as a last resort. After 1820, institutions were the preferred solution for problems such as insanity, delinquency, crime, and poverty. The asylum did not offer a benevolent escape for the mad, but a place to repress madness and enforce conformity. "The well-ordered asylum would exemplify the proper principles of social organization and thus insure the safety of the republic and promote its glory."[19]

The physical construction of asylums was greatly influenced by their medical superintendents. Some doctors boasted of a 100 percent cure rate for mental illness. Such projections of treatment success fueled the movement to build asylums. Also there existed competition among medical superintendents to report very high cure rates, and reformers wanted the United States to lead the Western world in this respect.

Control Becomes Treatment

The "science" of phrenology holds some important keys for understanding the development of psychiatry from 1820 to 1840. Most nineteenth-century British psychiatrists embraced phrenology because of its simple yet comprehensive explanation of human behavior. Further, phrenology located mental illness within the human physiology. Franz Gall, the "father" of phrenology, convinced most of his medical colleagues that the brain determined moral and intellectual qualities. Thus, medical treatments could be utilized to suppress the dysfunctions emanating from disturbed organs. Consequently, idleness or overactivity of the brain could be a determinant of insanity. By focusing on the structures of the brain, phrenologists led psychiatry to become a physiological science.[20] Stress could thus be placed on objective (rational) standards of measuring health and illness.

Toward the end of the nineteenth century, most European psychiatrists believed that physical health determined mental health. Mental disease was caused by morbid states of the nervous system and the brain. Because of this morbidity, mental health could not be restored by rational, psychological treatments. The purpose of treatment was to achieve an ideal physiological state so that the body could return to a perfect instrument of rational will.[21] And as medical technology progressed so, too, did the reliance on medical treatments.[22] Within the spirit of nineteenth-century positivism, the confinement of unreasonable people led to the development of a science that would restore reason. This science was predicated upon the assumptions of positivism and became the basis for measuring mental illness. Psychiatry, in a sense, sought legitimacy by becoming a modern science, predicated on the medical model of madness.

SOCIAL REACTIONS TO MENTAL ILLNESS: SCIENCE IS SOVEREIGN

At the beginning of the twentieth century, medical superintendents of state insane asylums were politically powerful and had a corner on the treatment market. Because these administrators wanted to correct past abuses, treatment was made scientific. Modern technologies were combined with the newest developments in physiology to produce what were thought to be progressive remedies for mental illness. Yet until the late 1940s, reactions to the insane were noncurative and nihilistic. That is, reason was stressed at the expense of asking questions about the social origins of illness. Through the technical manipulation of a person's physiology, madness was to be controlled.

Electroconvulsive Therapy and Psychosurgery

Two of the most popular physiological remedies for mental illness were electroconvulsive therapy (ECT) and psychosurgery. Although both are still practiced in private and public facilities, their use has declined since the introduction of medication.[23] ECT and psychosurgery soon moved beyond their "therapeutic" purpose and became instruments of threat, abuse, and punishment for nonconforming persons. Because of the invasive nature of these methods, it is argued that they offend the public. Furthermore, these two treatments are no longer used because it is unclear how they affect the mind and because pain is not supposed to accompany treatment. Today, both ECT and psychosurgery are used in conjunction with medication, although this was not always the case. Even with the use of medications, it became necessary to rely on another less "physical" remedy for mental disorders. Because the eroticism that is indigenous to the body tends to obscure reason, more rational solutions to madness had to be sought.

The Introduction of Drug Therapy

The introduction of lithium in 1948 and Thorazine in 1954 ushered in a new form of treatment for mental disorders.[24] By 1981, pharmacists were filling 154 million prescriptions for psychotropic drugs per year.[25] Because of the move to empty asylums, drugs became a "revolutionary"means of achieving deinstitutionalization. Since treatment in the community has been seen as the "least restrictive alternative," psychotropic medications became identified as a tool of liberation for the mentally ill.

In fact, psychopharmacology is particularly attractive to psychiatrists. Not only is the primary responsibility for mental illness turned over to physicians, but psychiatry is in the mainstream of medicine and science by relying on drugs. By making the diagnosis and treatment of mental illness consistent with procedures used in other medical disciplines, the image problems that have plagued the development of psychiatry can be overcome. Because drugs can be used easily to control patients, their use is consistent with persisting views of mental illness—that it needs to be repressed. The key premise of psychiatry is that mental disorders are indicative of illnesses. Once this is accepted, illnesses are reacted to as entities divorced from the person. The illness is treated and not the person. Thus, the problem becomes objectified, a step necessary for reason to be restored.

Drug therapy provides an important link between psychiatry and science. Controlling a mad person prior to the introduction of medications was very physical and personal. Psychiatrists had few options beyond restraint, seclusion, and some other physical means. Drugs, on the other hand, obscure the relationship between the body and the treatment. The body becomes the medium of treatment but not its focus. The individual does not have to be controlled as a person but, instead, can be approached in an objective, rational manner.

During the age of reason, psychiatry became a positive science. Thus, the scientists of reason were required to accomplish the following: first, define madness as a lack of reason; second, indicate how this lack of reason was an illness of the mind; and third, establish a science to cure the illness. Accordingly, madness became a "thing" and not a quality of human existence because positivism requires that all methods be empirical, objective, and reliable. Because positivism avoids humanistic and subjective concerns, psychiatry's quest to be scientific obscures the human and social experience of insanity.

Diagnosing Mental Disorders

Although preceded by two smaller and less technical versions, the *Diagnostic and Statistical Manual of Mental Disorders* (DSM-III) is the "state of the 'science' " in psychiatry. Most psychiatrists in the

United States utilize the DSM-III as their "bible" for classifying patients' disorders. The DSM-III represents the ultimate rationalization of human problems and thus embodies the most rigorous form of diagnostic reason because diagnoses are made according to a logical, precise, and objective procedure. The members of the task force that created this system have taken problems and classified them into 227 possible discrete diagnoses on five "axes."[26] The axis system allows for multiple diagnoses and a variety of information to be used in diagnosis and treatment.

Axes I, II, and III constitute the official diagnostic assessment. Included in these three are clinical syndromes, personality disorders, and physical disorders. Axes IV and V are available for use in "special clinical and research settings."[27] Included here are psychosocial factors and measures of adaptive functioning, such as social and occupational information. An examination of the five axes leads to the following conclusions: first, DMS-III is biased in favor of the medical or disease model of psychiatry, and, second, social problems become personal problems and thus an individual's responsibility. Although neither conclusion is startling, important implications follow in terms of how mental illness is understood.

By allowing the medical profession to define madness, this human problem is identified as indicative of pathology. By aligning themselves with physicians, psychiatrists can ignore the social side of "disease." Indeed, they can be scientists. Social change is not prescribed, while individual change is mandated. Madness is no longer a public problem to be accepted or tolerated, a "natural" state of human existence, but rather an illness of the mind. According to the disease model of madness, social reality is objective and distinguishes health from illness, while specifying the type of person therapy should produce.

As part of the rapidly increasing technology in medicine, the mad have been subjected to confinement, consolidation, electroconvulsive therapy, psychosurgery, and, finally, medication. These responses to and treatments for the mentally ill have attempted to suppress madness. The ultimate goal is to eliminate the individual's problem by whatever means are available. Although hindsight teaches that these responses to the mentally ill have often been cruel, dangerous, discriminatory, and painful, the medical model of madness is still embraced. It is often asserted, however, that humane relief from mental illness is possible with medications. Perhaps history will teach that medications simply dull persons' senses to a problem that is social and not merely physiological.

CONCLUSION

Madness, or mental illness, was first recognized as a social phenomenon. Individuals who were mad were not blamed or held responsible for their madness. Although they were not free from ridicule, the mad were tolerated in the community because madness was understood as part of social life. The classical era introduced a new conception of humans and of human responsibility. Because actors exercised free will in their activities, an individual's actions were thought to be either rational or irrational. Thus, questions of reason came to dominate discussions of mental illness.

Accompanying the classical age of reason was a secularization of thought. Divine causes of problems were rejected for more formal, objective, and scientific explanations. Thus, rational approaches to studying problems came to dominate philosophy and science. In fact, some might argue that rational thought became science. In the field of medicine generally, pathological physical states were identified as causes of disease. Psychiatry sought to apply this method to the study of mental disorders, thus bringing about the birth of mental illness. A concomitant social change was confinement of the poor, criminal, and insane, while placing them under the care of physicians. This era rendered mad persons as both sick and responsible for their illness, as mental illness became an individual phenomenon.

Essential to the development of modern psychiatry is the objectification of human problems. By assuming that scientific rationality is neutral, psychiatry separates "true from good, science from ethics."[28] To be considered a science, psychiatry had to rationalize illness; thus, pathology became an objective condition. In order to be objective, medical technologies were created that were treated as devoid of any values. However, technological development is a social process with *a priori* assumptions. For example, the goal of technology in the treatment of mental illness is control. Once recognized as an individual phenomenon, mental illness was defined as something that should be repressed. Hence, treatment becomes equated with securing social order. In point of fact, the rotary machine, confinement, restraint, ECT, psychosurgery, and medications are all technologies of control.

The rationalization and objectification of madness has some important implications for the study of mental illness. First, the identification of mental illness is done by technical experts. Why certain groups of people are overrepresented in asylums is not important to technicians because this is an ethical and political issue. Medicine has traditionally avoided such questions. Second, individualizing mental illness negates social prevention of madness. Because mental illness is perceived as an individual problem, the public does not have to assume responsibility for mental illness. Although some epidemiological studies show stratified patterns of mental illness, the response to this information is to focus all change at the individual level.[29] And third, the rationalization of mental illness means that cures occur on a case-by-case basis, rather than at a social or group level. Reduced in importance are the social conditions that may be causing a problem.

Establishing more humane responses to mental illness challenges all societies. For example, a humane response would reverse objectification. As opposed to the scientific approach to making diagnoses, a perspective that recognizes social responsibility for madness would raise new questions and offer new responses to mental illness. For example, the higher rates of schizophrenia among the poor could lead to conclusions about the inhumane conditions of poverty.[30] Rather than identifying the poor as "better candidates" for schizophrenia, a more humane and, perhaps, preventative social response would be to change the conditions of poverty.

A more humane response to the mentally ill does not require an abandonment of what is already known about mental illness. Furthermore, such a perspective does not suggest an abolition of psychiatry. Instead, mental illness must be returned to its social context, presented to society as a public problem, and responded to by changing the social conditions that exacerbate problems in daily living.

NOTES

1. For example, Lady Macbeth from *Macbeth* and the character Ophelia in *Hamlet*, by William Shakespeare (fifteenth century); the painting "Ship

of Fools," by Hieronymus Bosch (fifteenth century); and the main character in *Don Quixote* by Miguel de Cervantes (sixteenth century).

2. George Rosen, *Madness in Society: Chapters in the Historical Sociology of Mental Illness* (Chicago: University of Chicago Press, 1968), pp. 21–138.

3. Ibid., pp. 71–138.

4. Michel Foucault, *Madness and Civilization*, trans. Richard Howard (New York: Vintage Books, 1973), p. 64.

5. Ibid., pp. 3–37.

6. Ibid., p. 64.

7. Ibid., pp. 38–64.

8. Ibid., p. 45.

9. Ibid., p. 49.

10. Ibid., pp. 78–84.

11. Ibid., pp. 74–78.

12. Ibid., p. 74.

13. Ibid., p. 158.

14. A patient would be strapped into a chair that was attached to a movement device. The patient would then be spun around in circles at various speeds. The movement would force the "insane" matter in the body to be thrust outward.

15. Foucault, *Madness and Civilization*, pp. 159–177.

16. Ibid., p. 197.

17. Ibid., p. 250.

18. William F. Bynum, "Rationales of Therapy in British Psychiatry, 1780–1835," in Andrew T. Scull, ed., *Madhouses, Mad-Doctors, and Madmen* (Philadelphia: University of Pennsylvania Press, 1981), pp. 35–57.

19. David Rothman, *The Discovery of the Asylum: Social Order and Disorder in the New Republic* (Boston: Little, Brown, 1971), p. xix.

20. Roger Cooter, "Phrenology and British Alienists, 1825–1845," in Scull, *Madhouses, Mad-Doctors, and Madmen*, pp. 58–104.

21. Michael J. Clark, "The Rejection of Psychological Approaches to Mental Disorder in Late Nineteenth-Century British Psychiatry," in Scull, *Madhouses, Mad-Doctors, and Madmen*, pp. 271–312.

22. John Marshall Townsend, *Cultural Conceptions of Mental Illness: A Comparison of Germany and America* (Chicago: University of Chicago Press, 1978).

23. Mark J. Mills et al., "Electroconvulsive Therapy in Massachusetts," *American Journal of Psychiatry* 14 (April 1984): 534; Jules Older, "Psychosurgery: Ethical Issues and a Proposal for Control," *American Journal of Orthopsychiatry* 44, no. 5 (October 1974): 661.

24. William C. Cockerham, *Sociology of Mental Disorder* (Englewood Cliffs, N.J.: Prentice-Hall, 1981).

25. R. M. Restak, "Psychiatry in America," *The Wilson Quarterly* 7, no. 4 (Autumn 1983): 94.

26. Robert L. Spitzer, *Diagnostic and Statistical Manual of Mental Disorders*, 3d ed. (Washington, D.C.: American Psychiatric Association, 1980).

27. Ibid., p. 8.

28. Herbert Marcuse, *One-Dimensional Man* (Boston: Beacon Press, 1964), p. 146.

29. Robert E. Lee Faris and H. Warren Dunham, *Mental Disorders in Urban Areas: An Ecological Study of Schizophrenia and Other Psychoses* (Chicago: University of Chicago Press, 1939); August B. Hollingshead and Frederick C. Redlich, *Social Class and Mental Illness: A Community Study* (New York: John Wiley and Sons, 1958).

30. Faris and Dunham, *Mental Disorders in Urban Areas*.

6

The Invasion of the Female Body

Esther S. Merves

This chapter will analyze how technology has taken possession of the human body and thus has usurped the needs of human beings.[1] As has been discussed elsewhere, technology should be understood only in terms of how it is used by humans.[2] Nonetheless, as Herbert Marcuse notes, although technology cannot be isolated from the use to which it is put, the technological society has become a system of domination that represses the citizenry.[3]

The technological world consists of objectivity and numerical measurement, while technology refers to the social application of scientific knowledge. What distinguishes technology or science from other types of knowledge is its alleged objectivity, thus suggesting that a universal knowledge exists that is divorced from social experience or subjectivity. Objective knowledge is considered to be distinct from social experience and thus ahistorical. In other words, its ontological base refers to "things" that can be measured numerically or dissected analytically apart from human perception and social interpretation. Thus, scientific objects exist absolutely and are "untainted" by human experience.

Medical technology, in the form of scientific knowledge, treats the human body as an objective phenomenon, differentiated from human or personal experience. Simply put, the body and the person are viewed as two separate entities, the objective and subjective. The objective has a life of its own, because scientific laws allegedly govern its behavior. Moreover, each part of the body operates according to its own laws, as witnessed by the proliferation of medical specialties. Michel Foucault refers to this as "technology of the flesh," in that the body is deprived of its human dimension and treated as a self-equilibrating organism.[4] Ivan Illich refers to this as "medicalizing" social life, for bodily experiences are invalid unless medically verified.[5] In other words, medical science informs persons of how they feel, as opposed to corroborating their social experiences. Because social experience is not considered important in the scientific model, technology eliminates the human dimension of the body. Menstruation, for example, is not defined or interpreted directly from women's experiences but rather by an abstract scientific (objective) nosology.

The invasion of the female body refers to the structuring of the female body through artificial determinations. It stands for ideational or physical acts that turn against humanity and, in particular, women.[6] Technology has reduced the female to biological and social functions that she can neither reject nor transcend; her body is her vulnerability and she is continually subject to physical and psychological control by others.[7] The social management of menstruation shall be considered exemplary of this invasion, while what passes for scientific knowledge about menstruation, what its consequences have been and how this information has given women a distorted image of their bodies will be discussed. Finally, in discussing prospects for using technology responsibly, an alternative philosophical and social position for evaluating menstruation will be offered.

THE SOCIAL CONTEXT

Before examining how technology deanimates the body, the social context in which this occurs must be recognized. Because women occupy a relatively powerless position, they have little access to social resources. Women are dependent upon men for political representation, economic support, social position, physical protection, and psychological approval. To maintain this political status quo, however, it is necessary to control what people think. There are many means of socialization whereby this is accomplished: education, religion, and the mass media. With women, covert mechanisms of control have been more successful than with most other oppressed groups.[8] In other words, due to the perceived normalcy and legitimacy of sex roles, women have been controlled with little opposition. This is especially relevant to the technological control of women's bodies through medicine because the authority of medical science is legitimated by its claim to objectivity. Thus, science serves as an extremely powerful yet silent (unquestioned) means of social control.

A perusal of the sex-role and socialization literature reveals that females are characterized by the same traits as the victimized groups that Gordon Allport studied in *The Nature of Prejudice*, in addition to the Indians under British rule and the Algerians under the French.[9] The female image is characterized as small, weak, soft, light, dull, peaceful, relaxed, cold, rounded, passive, and slow.[10] Other characterizations often include: uncertain, anxious, nervous, hasty, careless, childish, helpless, sorry, timid, clumsy, stupid, silly, and domestic.[11]

That women are to be beautiful playthings and sexual objects for men in exchange for security and love determines their prospects for mobility and the way in which they use their bodies; in other words, the dimensions of their physical freedom.[12] The resulting obsession with beauty perpetuates what Patricia Hampl calls the "beauty disease," which characterizes the feminine way of life as primarily the pursuit of beauty.[13] As Andrea Dworkin notes:

Women should be beautiful. All repositories of cultural wisdom from King Solomon to King Hefner agree: women should be beautiful. It is the reverence for female beauty which informs the romantic ethos, gives it its energy and justification. Beauty is transformed into that golden ideal. Beauty—rapturous and abstract. Women must be beautiful and Woman is Beauty.[14]

But because women are not born beautiful, they must be made into beauties by creams, lotions, dyes, and with the the help of special tools. And no part of the female is left untouched:

No feature or extremity is spared the art, or pain, of improvement. Hair is dyed, lacquered, straightened, permanented; eyebrows are plucked, penciled, dyed; eyes are lined, mascaraed, shadowed; lashes are curled or false— from head to toe, every feature of a woman's face, every section of her body, is subject to modification, alteration. This alteration is an ongoing, repetitive process. It is vital to the economy, the major substance of male-female role differentiation, the most immediate physical and psychological reality of being a woman. From the age of 11 or 12 until she dies, a woman will spend a large part of her time, money, and energy on binding, plucking, and deodorizing herself.[15]

Thus, beauty is really a mask to cover undesirable yet human qualities. The pain of beauty is part of womanhood, whether it results from footbinding, high heels, plucked eyebrows, shaved legs, surgical additions or removals. The pursuit of beauty epitomizes the invasion of the female body.

Just as women follow the rituals of beauty as an unquestioned aspect of everyday life, the dictates of medical science are given immense power because it represents a style of reason that transcends the limits of individual experience, religion, and tradition. Because science is allegedly based upon truth and scientific facts it can control behavior without question. This is exemplified in the scientific studies of menstruation.

THE SOCIAL MANAGEMENT OF MENSTRUATION

The social management of menstruation will refer to the organization of scientific knowledge regarding the menstrual cycle, the social consequences of this knowledge for women, and women's experiences with their bodies when mediated by science.

The Organization of Scientific Knowledge regarding the Menstrual Cycle

It is necessary to begin with a general theoretical proposition: Any knowledge set mediated by an existing social structure will tend to reproduce that structure.[16] Thus, it should be no surprise that there is little information available on the female's experiences of menstruation. Although women experience up to 500 menstrual cycles in a lifetime, a shroud of secrecy and silence exists around the subject of menstruation. It is still connected with ideas of horror, danger, shame, and sin.[17] Not even the reemergence of the women's movement during the 1970s has altered the perception of menstruation as unclean, unsafe, and undesirable.

A sociological perspective is notably absent from this body of scientific literature as most menstrual studies relate to psychosomatic medicine and are dominated by the medical model with its focus on pain and discomfort. Neither the models nor theories of the menstrual cycle have been clearly articulated, although a multitude of hypotheses has been tested with contradictory and conflicting results.[18] The traditional viewpoints attempt to predict the female personality, psychology, and behavior from menstrual cycle phases (measurement still debated among physicians), particularly hostility or anxiety. Even the social approaches are more psychological than sociological and focus mostly on explaining persons' attitudes toward menstrual sickness. Only within the last few years has there been a demand for research relevant to women's experiences.[19]

Most research still centers on the outdated nature versus nurture debate. In spite of this, studies on language, attitudes, labeling, and the transmission of menstrual knowledge point to the need for a broader perspective on menstruation. For example, V. Ernster found numerous differences between males and females in their use of negative menstrual euphemisms.[20] Furthermore, she found that females learn the various terms for menstruation from their mothers or other females at the time of menarche, while males learn them in high school and college from male peers and use them in a context (and in effect transmit a menstrual sex taboo) to denote a woman's sexual unavailability or to degrade another male. Thus, there are socialized differences in the meaning of menstruation. When euphemisms are transmitted, social meanings and expectations are also generated. M. Chernovetz found different responses by the same respondents to identical questionnaires when one was labeled with the term "menstrual."[21] Specifically, respondents were less likely to report distress on the menstrual questionnaire than on one assessing general health. Diane Ruble experimentally manipulated women's perceptions of their menstrual cycle phase and found that learned associations lead them to overestimate or exaggerate their symptoms.[22] In characterizing women's personalities, Randi Koeske and Gary Koeske found that a significant proportion of negative ratings were given when a woman was said to be exhibiting premenstrual symptoms, regardless of other available information.[23] However, situational factors were discounted and biology emphasized when explaining negative but not positive moods as respondents rated hypothetical cases. Results from attitude studies reveal a strong difference between male and female attitudes toward menstruation. What all of the above studies have in common is the inclusion of social factors as mediating the interpretation of menstruation. However, these studies are not considered as authoritative as those produced by medical science. The majority of menstrual studies in the medical field exclude the factors of human intentionality and meaning. Thus, the findings reported above are not disseminated as widely as "pure" medical research.

The preponderance of research originating in medical or psychiatric settings focuses largely on symptoms, such as pain, discomfort, anxiety, or hostility, while the menstrual cycle itself is considered ontologically autonomous. This is to say, it is hoped that laws will be discovered by studying the menstrual cycle that will explain pain or anxiety. Scientific laws, in other words, are assumed to determine women's experiences with their bodies. However, a review of these medical studies reveals no evidence for increased cyclic complaints, while the evidence for emotional change is more conflicting than is generally recognized.[24] Furthermore, the existence of a class of behaviors that fluctuate with changes in the menstrual cycle has not been demonstrated.[25] This hodgepodge of studies has produced no firm evidence. Generally, menstrual research treats menstruation as either producing no alterations in behavior or emotions or as a terrible, disruptive force in normal life, as exemplified by M. E. Ivey and Judith Bardwick's conclusion, "The menstrual cycle exercises gross influence on female behavior."[26]

It is important to refer back to the opening statement that any knowledge set may reproduce the existing social structure. Therefore, some of the following questions should be asked about this research. Who benefits from this research? In what context is it conducted? Why do menstrual taboos continue to exist? Who benefits from maintaining these definitions? Clearly, the prevailing views on menstruation are fundamental to sustaining the asymmetrical relations between women and men as they supply a covert means of social control under the guise of medical knowledge. Therefore, a broader perspective is needed on this problem than is offered by science and technology.

The Consequences Women Face as a Social Group

The scientific work on menstruation supports the view that women are specially handicapped by their biology.[27] This reproductive machine model of the body contends that female behavior can be explained in terms of uterine physiology. Although some research has successfully challenged this view, other derogatory beliefs about menstruation remain intact. In fact, because most research is still predicated on the nature versus nurture controversy, it cannot offer a real alternative.

The menstrual taboo that portrays menstruating women as corrupt and unclean is a part of medical theories, religious beliefs, and even current social attitudes and suggests that menstruation is a disease and menstruating women should hide this fact when afflicted.[28] Freudians conceive menstrual blood to be the symbol of the woman's lost penis. By forbidding her to touch utensils shared with men and prohibiting sexual relations, the man is supposedly not reminded of his primal castration and does not have to witness the result of the woman's castration.[29]

Victorians generally believed that menstruation was a disease that made all women invalids for much of their lives. Accordingly, menstruating women were thought to be incapable of physical or intellectual exertion. Ashley Montagu reported that in mid–nineteenth-century France, menstruating women were barred from wine making, mushroom picking, silkworm tending, and sugar refining in order to safeguard these products. In 1878, a British medical journal reported that hams became spoiled because menstruating women had cured them. Even as late as 1920, it was reported that freshly cut flowers wilted faster when handled by menstruating women.[30] Also, menstruation was the reason given by physicians as to why women could not expect to live the same style of life as men.[31]

The impact of this scientific knowledge has been the construction of an image of women as unreliable reproductive machines in addition to erratic workers and unstable mothers. Additionally, the view prevails that women cannot be trusted because they have poor control over their emotions. Menstruation, when viewed as a debilitating handicap, has been used to bar women from employment because factories pose a threat to women's "sacred" reproductive capacity. Ironically, they also have been barred from these same activities because they were seen as a pollutant that threatens industry. Employers still continue to cite women's unsuitability for technically demanding work.[32]

Doctors often define women as troublesome patients. Yet women who suffer from painful menses have been told one of two things by doctors: It is all in your head, and/or, even if the pain seems real, it is part of your inheritance as a woman so live with it.[33] A recent study of gynecologists reveals that most believe that menstrual difficulties result from improper attitude.[34] This is in spite of the fact that ninety percent of all women experience some form of menstrual pain. Yet this finding may explain why only a fraction of these women ever seek professional help for painful menses.

Another group that benefits from these notions is the multimillion dollar menstrual products industry, which tells women to hide their monthly problem. This is the most common theme in menstrual advertising along with the claim that menstruation produces discomfort and is unpleasant. Many products are marketed with the slogan of "no show—no smell." Young (emphasis on youth) women are dressed in white or light colors in ads and are often shown emerging from the shower. Menstruation is dirty, smelly, and shameful for women, but very profitable for the Tampax and Kotex corporations. These marketing campaigns have become even more aggressive over the last few years, for now women are told that their bodies emit unpleasant secretions not only during menstruation but every day.

Women have to face discrimination, humiliation, and degradation because science has defined their bodies as a monster with a mind of its own. Medical science defines women's experiences, rather than recognizing them. Simply put, the female body is reduced to an objective condition and severed from experience. Women's sensations, feelings, attitudes or, in other words, their intersubjective life is not considered to be valid.

Women's Experiences

How do these images and body of knowledge affect women's perception of menstruation? How is menstruation experienced? How does empirical reality reflect the invasion of the female body? To this end, the social construction of the menstrual experience will be discussed. The data used were gleaned from in-depth interviews of sixty women representing a wide variety of ages (from twenty-one to fifty-five) and lifestyles.[35] Below are some of the general themes revealed in these interviews.

The data show that women base their interpretations of menstruation on what they believe to be scientific knowledge. Their experience mirrors the types of research mentioned earlier in that menstruation is thought inevitably to produce discomfort, is an acceptable explanation for mood or behavioral changes, and plays a role in altering sexual relations and purchasing habits.

A very common experience for women is for a male to ask them if they are menstruating. This is usually taken as an insult by the woman. The question "Are you on the rag?" is supposed to account for something a woman has said or done that does not fit into the male's definition of reality. This is an example of what Jurgen Habermas refers to as distorted communication, which reflects an unequal distribution of power.[36] Furthermore, spouses or male friends usually relate to menses as an illness or as a cause of sexual disruption. These attitudes relate directly to how a woman experiences her sexuality during menstruation. Since most women report experiencing heightened bodily awareness, this may be interpreted as a desire for both more and less sexual contact or affection. In fact, a pervasive theme pertains to women noting an increase in sexual desire but a withdrawal from sexual activity by choice or because of an unwilling partner. As mentioned earlier, menstruation may be considered a sexual liability from a male point of view. Other studies find a similar pattern: Males find menstruation much more distasteful and they hold more stereotypical beliefs about menstruation than women.[37] Some women reported that their mates hold extremely negative, patronizing, or even hostile attitudes toward menstruation.

Another theme related to the impact of technology is that menstruation is seen as a biological or scientific process. When asked how they would explain menstruation to a premenstrual adolescent, women overwhelmingly state they would stress that it is a biological event. In other words, the scientific view is dominant.

Not surprisingly, because the study by Esther Merves adopts a qualitative approach and focuses on the meaning of menstruation, a great deal of variability is present because not all women viewed menstruation as a handicap. Although a sizable portion of the women interviewed altered their daily routine and dress during menstruation, not all of these changes were due to negative feelings. Some women reported feeling more creative and productive. In fact, a heightened sense of consciousness may occur in a variety of activities. Interpretation of the menstrual scent is also highly variable, contrary to the strong message conveyed by the medical profession. Some descriptions include the adjectives "normal," "sweet," "heavy," or "none at all."

What can be made from these data? Women see menstruation as a scientific process confronting them, rather than something that is socially constructed and maintained intersubjectively. Moreover, women are highly vulnerable to male definitions that reinforce the messages present in the media. The crux of the matter is that they often do not feel like themselves. They adopt a medical view rather than a human one. Their everyday lives (the words used to refer to menstruation, conversations, interaction during menstruation, the "sexual" problem) reflect the existing state of technology that is dehumanizing and irresponsive to human needs. It is assumed that some baseline human experience should exist that is objective and determined physiologically (scientifically). Consequently, menstruation represents an aberration, as technology perpetrates a distorted view of women's experiences. It leads women to experience menstruation as something outside of normal life they should hide or fear. This technological or scientific view of menstruation perpetuates male domination of and discrimination against women.

FUTURE PROSPECTS

Currently, menstruation is treated as a phenomenon that exists outside human experience because it is an objective or physiological condition. Knowledge about the menstrual cycle is thought to exist *sui generis*, neatly packaged and waiting to be discovered by modern technology. In order to change this state of affairs, it must be recognized that the experience of menstruation is a social construction, a human conception that attempts to provide social life with order in the face of its biological absence.[38] Yet the scientific construction, parading as objective knowledge, reflects an imbalance in power among men and women. Accordingly, technology also must be recognized as a social construction as opposed to representing universal truth. In this way, technology cannot be used as a tool of social or sexual repression.

The next step is to subvert another myth that sustains technology, the nature versus nurture debate. As Karen Callaghan and John Murphy trenchantly reveal, this debate has been undermined because the existence of human nature is now understood to be questionable. It is worth quoting from their treatise, which is based on recent developments in philosophy, biology, and anthropology:

Human nature can no longer be understood to be a fundamental constraint to human action which can be superficially modified by socialization, but rather is an openness which must be stabilized through the effort of social institutions which are formulated by social (human) action. . . . Human existence does not merely inhabit or have a body, but much more fundamentally embodies a body.[39]

Thus, to conceptualize menstruation as a biological process, and human experience as something that reacts to it, is erroneous. To assume that menstruation is akin to a closed system that follows a course of its own (a biological process) and limits (as if it exerts a force) the range of human experience is to assume there exists some "basic stuff" that determines the boundaries of human existence. When this conceptualization is rendered obsolete, what is to take its place? Once again, as Callaghan and Murphy explain:

With these new advances, as Marcuse suggests, biological and social life must be understood to be a "project" (Sartre's term), whereby the entire corpus of existence itself is viewed to be a human (historical or cultural) determination. Accordingly, there is no longer thought to be any "basic stuff" which specifies what is humanly possible, but instead a type of "world openness" which must be filled in by human action for human existence to have a form.[40]

Yet what does this mean in terms of understanding the human body in particular and society in general? As Max Weber and Jean-Paul Sartre suggest, behavior should be interpreted with reference to human actions and goals:

The social world is defined by human goals; indeed, it is the fact that matter is worked upon by human desires and labor which gives us a world that is intelligible. . . . Social structures, whether they appear as "stimuli," "results," "circumstances," "processess" or "conditions" (Weber), or as "tools," "instruments" or "material situations" (Sartre), should be defined in relation to a human undertaking.[41]

Menstrual research has ignored the individual as an actress in the social world who defines the reality she encounters. Thus, the traditional theoretical conceptualization of menstruation and consequent methodologies are inadequate because they assert that action is determined by external and constraining nonsocial forces, such as universal psychological factors or reified physiological constructs.

By utilizing an action frame of reference, which incorporates the work of Weber, Alfred Schutz,[42] Peter Berger and Thomas Luckmann,[43] Herbert Blumer,[44] and others, positivistic (technological) explanations are rejected and concern is directed toward human action, which creates meanings that are socially sustained and changed. The technological image of the body, however, ignores human action as the basis of meaning and instead posits a deterministic model based on so-called objective facts.

Modern writers argue that experience of the world is incoherent unless it is organized through social actions. In other words, personal realities are constructed by interpersonal processes. Socially shared beliefs specify the kinds of interpretations open to women for defining their experiences. According to Schutz:

the world of "daily life" is an intersubjective world which existed long before our birth, was experienced and interpreted by others, our predecessors, as an organized world. Now it is given to our experience and interpretation. All interpretation of this world is based upon a stock of previous experiences of it, our own experiences, and those handed down to us by our parents and teachers, which in the form of "knowledge at hand" function as a scheme of reference.[45]

Berger and Luckman, like Schutz, illustrate the world to have multiple realities, some of which are apprehended routinely, while others present individuals with problems of one kind or another.[46] Most important, however, each order of social reality has its own special and separate style of existence.

Menstruation can be considered to constitute a finite province of meaning. Finite provinces of meaning are social realities within the paramount reality, marked by unique meanings and modes of experience.[47] Thus, a finite province of meaning refers to a set of experiences that reveal a specific cognitive style in addition to a particular form of sociality.[48] Schutz takes special care to emphasize that it is the meaning of the experience and not the ontological structure of the objects which constitutes reality. Accordingly, it is not menstruation as a biological or scientific (technological) process that is important but rather it is the meaning or the experience of menstruation that constitutes social reality. Bodily experiences should not be objectified as scientific facts that reflect universal laws. Instead, the body must be interpreted rather than explained technolgically.

As a menstruating species, humans are free from the constraints imposed by sexual behavior that is completely determined by ovulation. Thus, menstruation, as an experience, is channeled in specific directions socially, rather than biologically. As Callaghan and Murphy write:

Human nature is fundamentally open and a human creation. . . . These new theories contend that even the supposedly most basic elements of existence are created, and not merely altered, by human action. Human action is, therefore, now conceived to be the ground of existence itself, and not merely a force which can supplement some assumed "basic stuff" of life.[49]

In order to unite technology with its human origin, women must, as Dworkin suggests, radically redefine the nature of their bodies. "The body must be freed, liberated, quite literally: from paint and girdles and all varieties of crap. Women must stop mutilating their bodies and *start living in them*."[50]

SUMMARY

Technology has invaded the female body in the form of scientific knowledge. This invasion by science distorts women's experiences because their bodies are objectified and reified. Science defines the human body (menstruation) as an entity that has an objective status and determines behavior. This is a version of the notion "biology is destiny," which has been used to oppress women and minorities. Yet science and technology are touted as apolitical because oppression is accomplished covertly, which is preferable to overt acts of force. By recognizing the social ground of action and that bodily changes do not have inherent significance but rather a socially constructed meaning, human beings will be able to experience their bodies more freely.

NOTES

1. Frankfurt Institute of Social Research, *Aspects of Sociology* (Boston: Beacon Press, 1956), p. 94.

2. Gila Hayim, *The Existential Sociology of Jean-Paul Sartre* (Amherst: University of Massachusetts Press, 1980), p. 8.

3. Herbert Marcuse, *One-Dimensional Man* (Boston: Beacon Press, 1964), p. 16.

4. Michel Foucault, *The History of Sexuality*, trans. Robert Hurley, vol. 1 (New York: Pantheon Books, 1978).

5. Ivan Illich, *Limits to Medicine* (New York: Penguin Books, 1976).

6. Hayim, *Existential Sociology*, p. 8.

7. Anne Koedt, Ellen Levine, and Anita Rapone, *Radical Feminism* (New York: Quadrangle, 1973), p. 407.

8. Ibid., p. 139.

9. Ibid., p. 141.

10. Ibid., p. 149.

11. Ibid., p. 140.

12. Andrea Dworkin, *Woman Hating* (New York: Dutton, 1974), p. 113.

13. Patricia Hampl, *A Romantic Education* (Boston: Houghton Mifflin, 1981), p. 86.

14. Dworkin, *Woman Hating*, p. 112.

15. Ibid., p. 113.

16. T. R. Young, *Information, Ideology and Political Reality* (Livermore, Colo.: Red Feather Institute, 1982), p. 5.

17. Rina Grafstein, "Menstruation and Sexuality: An Attitudinal Survey," *Canadian Women Studies* 3, no. 2 (Winter 1981): 14–16.

18. P. Slade, "Menstrual Cycle Symptoms in Infertile and Control Subjects: A Re-evaluation of the Evidence for Psychological Changes," *Journal of Psychosomatic Research* 25, no. 3 (May/June 1981): 175–181. Also see Barbara Sommer, "Models of Menstrual Stress: Incidence and Specificity," in Alice J. Dan, Effie A. Graham, and Carol P. Beecher, eds., *The Menstrual Cycle: A Synthesis of Interdisciplinary Research* (New York: Springer, 1980), pp. 26–43.

19. Paula Weideger, *Menstruation and Menopause: Physiology, Psychology, Myth and Realtiy* (New York: Delta, 1977).

20. V. Ernster, "American Menstrual Expressions," *Sex Roles: A Journal of Research* 1 (January 1975): 3–13.

21. M. Chernovetz, W. Hones, and R. Hannsson, "Predictability, Attentional Focus, Sex Role Orientation, and Menstrual-Related Stress," *Psychosomatic Medicine* 41, no. 5 (August 1979): 383–391.

22. Diane N. Ruble, "Premenstrual Symptoms: A Reinterpretation," *Science* 197 (July 15, 1977): 291–292.

23. Randi K. Koeske and Gary F. Koeske, "An Attributional Approach to Moods and the Menstrual Cycle," *Journal of Personality and Social Psychology* 31, no. 3 (March 1975): 473–478.

24. Slade, "Menstrual Cycle Symptoms in Infertile and Control Subjects."

25. Juanita H. Williams, *Psychology of Women: Behavior in a Biosocial Context* (New York: Norton, 1983), p. 57.

26. M. E. Ivey and Judith M. Bardwick, "Patterns of Affective Fluctuation in the Menstrual Cycle," *Psychosomatic Medicine* 30, no. 3 (May/June 1968): 345.

27. Ann Oakley, *Subject Women* (New York: Pantheon, 1981), p. 121.

28. Bonnie K. Sloane, "News in Brief," *National Organization for Women Times* (January-February 1982): 4.

29. Weideger, *Menstruation and Menopause*, pp. 107–110.

30. Rita E. Montgomery, "A Cross-Cultural Study of Menstruation, Menstrual Taboos, and Related Social Variables," *Ethos*, 2 (Summer 1974): 137–176.

31. Oakley, *Subject Women*, p. 56.

32. Ibid., p. 57.

33. Sloane, "News in Brief," p. 4.

34. Grafstein, "Menstruation and Sexuality," pp. 14–16.

35. Esther Merves, "The Social Management of Menstruation," unpublished paper (Ohio State University, 1983).

36. Gibson Burrell and Gareth Morgan, *Sociological Paradigms and Organisational Analysis* (London: Heineman, 1979), p. 295.

37. J. Brooks, D. Ruble, and A. Clark, "College Women's Attitudes and Expectations concerning Menstrual Related Changes," *Psychosomatic Medicine* 39, no. 5 (September/October 1977), pp. 288–297.

38. Karen Callaghan and John Murphy, "A New View of an Old Issue: Human Nature and Social Institutions," unpublished paper (Ohio State University), p. 7.

39. Ibid., pp. 1, 7.

40. Ibid., p. 3.

41. Hayim, *Existential Sociology*, p. 9.

42. Alfred Schutz, *The Problem of Social Reality: Collected Papers*, ed. Maurice Natanson, vol. 1 (Netherlands: Martinus Nijhoff, 1973).

43. Peter L. Berger and Thomas Luckmann, *The Social Construction of Reality: A Treatise in the Sociology of Knowledge* (New York: Doubleday, 1967).

44. Herbert Blumer, *Symbolic Interactionism: Perspective and Method* (Englewood Cliffs, N.J.: Prentice Hall, 1969).

45. Schutz, *Problem of Social Reality*, p. 208.
46. Berger and Luckmann, *Social Construction*, p. 20.
47. Ibid., p. 24.
48. Schutz, *Problem of Social Reality*, p. 232.
49. Callaghan and Murphy, "A New View," p. 10.
50. Dworkin, *Women Hating*, p. 116 (emphasis added).

7

The Growth and Control of Medical Technology

Larry A. Nuttbrock

Modern medicine is under a reign of technology.[1] Because the science of medicine assumes that diseases can be analyzed independently of social and psychological considerations, technology submits these processes to ever-increasing degrees of diagnostic scrutiny.[2] With the introduction of the stethoscope and, more recently, X-ray machines and Computer-Assisted Tomography (CAT) scans, the inner recesses of the body can be probed, measured, and photographed. Indeed, the spectre of a high-technology medicine in which all parts of the body are observed, repaired, or replaced is no longer a matter of idle speculation.[3]

While organ transplants and other exotic techniques are still relatively rare, many elaborate techniques are now used on a routine basis. An armamentarium of electronic gadgetry and monitoring devices is customarily used during childbirth. When the problems of modern living cause stress, an array of mood-altering drugs is available. During the dying process, analgesics combat pain, psychodepressant drugs numb awareness, and a variety of life-support systems can maintain life almost indefinitely.[4]

From a medical point of view, the benefits of this technology are not obvious. A variety of studies points to the dubious nature of these medical practices. For example, infant mortality is mostly a function of nutrition. Actually, highly sophisticated neonatal care units have negligible effects on infant survival.[5] Also, the value of lifesaving machines is overestimated, while the complications resulting from their use raises compelling medical, social, and ethical issues.[6]

The problem with medical technology is not simply its ineffectiveness, but that it often causes disease. Iatrongenic, or "doctor made" diseases are those that result from medical care itself.[7] Ivan

on tests and machines to obtain and process information may lose the ability to make adequate clinical judgments, particularly when encountering novel situations. Additionally, technology may result in the "deskilling" of medical work because the social organization of technology tends to promote an inflexible approach to clinical practice. Stanley Reiser, for instance, cites physicians who complain that it is difficult in some hospitals to order a simple test for a specific diagnosis simply because it has become a routine practice to use an entire battery of tests.

Other writers stress the political side of health care. The underlying significance of political-economic factors in the spread of technology is best conveyed by noting that the health care industry spends $6,000 a year per physician to promote their products.[21] Certainly, health care in America is big business, with very high profit rates witnessed in this sector.[22]

Central to the critiques of the proliferation of technology sketched above is its effect on a person's definition and perception of reality, which has immense social and economic implications. After an examination of traditional attempts to control technology, a broader, essentially phenomenological, analysis of medical technology will be suggested.

CURRENT APPROACHES TO THE CONTROL OF MEDICAL TECHNOLOGY

The preceding discussion serves as a prelude to the following question: How should medical technology be controlled? Sparked in large part by skyrocketing medical costs, which are primarily a result of technological growth, social critics maintain that medical technology is currently applied in an inefficient, haphazardous, and often inhumane manner. There is little agreement, however, concerning the rationale for this misuse of technology. One school of thought maintains that medical technology and scientific medicine are intrinsically detrimental to health. According to this view, technology should be eliminated from the practice of medicine altogether. This viewpoint is held by Illich. Following from his notion of "structural iatrogenesis," health will be improved by reducing the use of technology as much as possible.

The problem with this view is the assumption on which it is based:

Medical technology is intrinsically deleterious. But it is not necessarily true that the "best medicine is always the least medicine" or that a return to prescientific medicine is the most propitious course to follow, for many drugs and procedures serve to promote health. The problem with medical technology is not its nature but its inappropriate use. Therefore, technology must be controlled and not abandoned.

If the spread of technology is to be controlled in a positive sense, how should this control be institutionalized socially? To answer this question, the discussion must now turn to the two principal means of medical control—professionalization and bureaucratization. Yet it will become clear that both of these models of social organization are problematic.

The Bureaucratic Control of Medical Technology

Although the writings of medical heretics such as Robert Mendelsohn along with social critics such as Illich have generated considerable debate, the notion of dismantling scientific-technological medicine is seldom seriously entertained. Instead, bureaucracy has been invoked as a means of rationally controlling technology.

Bureaucracy is a means of organizing work whereby tasks are assigned according to a formally prescribed division of labor that is designed to promote the goals of an organization. Efficiency is, in theory, maximized by routinizing the work process; that is, by dividing tasks into functionally related units and thereby controlling workers by assigning them particular tasks and positions in an organization.

Furthermore, the bureaucratic control of technology is based on rational criteria, such as cost, efficiency, proper allocation, and equity. This rational-bureaucratic approach to medical control is, on the surface, almost impossible to criticize. Given the extravagant cost of using technology, measures must be taken to ensure that those who use it derive some benefit. Thus, attempts must be made to formalize utilization criteria in order to guarantee that these guidelines are followed. After all, considering the recent increase in kidney transplants and the demand for donors, a national clearing house would certainly be useful for matching donors with recipients. And, given the belief that health care is a right, every pre-

from serious consideration the broader social implications of any decisions. How can a parent argue for the death of a permanently impaired child when scientific evidence indicates that the brain is functioning? How can a family of a heart patient argue against surgery when an electrocardiogram reveals a myocardial infarction? Simply put, the belief in and use of such technical bench marks precludes ethical considerations.

Also eliminated from scrutiny are the issues of power and exploitation that surround medical decisions. The use of medical technology routinely entails the exercise of power and influence over patients by practitioners, although this goes unnoticed because a neutral or technological means of domination is used. But as writers in the critical theory tradition note, the control of persons by technology, in the final analysis, represents the suppression of some individuals by others. This dictum applies also to medicine. It must be remembered that physicians are not necessarily personally or financially disinterested purveyors of medical knowledge and technology. A physician's advice to perform heart bypass surgery, for example, may be couched in technical terms, but his or her judgments are affected by the remuneration involved.[28]

In sum, a reliance on bureaucratic controls as a means of promoting both the rational and humanistic utilization of medical technology is fundamentally flawed. The holistic nature of health and illness is distorted, the values inherent in medical decisions are rendered opaque, and issues of power and domination tend to be overlooked. Science, technology, and bureaucracy operate on the same positivistic assumptions. Consequently, bureaucratic control of technology is an extension and further entrenchment of science and technology.

The Professional Control of Medical Technology

If health and illness are difficult to define in quantitative terms, why not allow physicians to use their "professional judgment" to make such determinations? In point of fact, if physicians are supposedly trained to treat the "whole patient," they should be in a position to preserve the human side of medical practice. If problems exist relative to the abuse of professional power, certainly the American Medical Association will punish all violators.

Following the classic definition of professions offered by Talcott Parsons and other structural functionalists, professionalization should be able to control the misuse of technology.[29] Professionals are viewed as personally disinterested purveyors of knowledge that only they understand. Also, professionals are described as a community of colleagues who accept the main values of society and are committed to promoting those values in their work. The relationship between professional and client is based on these values and not personal gain. Finally, the professions are assumed to be self-policing and exercise control over their members to guarantee they exhibit professional demeanor at all times.

If only these theoretically derived notions resembled what actually occurs during the practice of medicine! The underlying logic of this functionalist viewpoint is basically flawed, for society is not necessarily sustained by universal values. This style of theorizing, specifically the belief that the medical profession acts in a socially responsible manner, is best viewed as an ideology. As Eliot Freidson describes in his well-documented and scathing analysis of the medical profession, the perception that physicians exercise control over one another to promote the public good is an illusion.[30] Freidson writes that doctors are seldom in a position to observe one another's "nonprofessional" behavior and, even if such observations are made, beyond widely publicized cases of gross negligence, the likelihood is small that any peer sanctioning will occur.

But the medical profession is based on another illusion: that health and illness can be defined biochemically and that medical knowledge describes these processes objectively. Just as bureaucracies tend to promote definitions of health and illness that are consistent with the logic of this type of organization, medical professionals also construct a medical "reality" instead of interpreting symptoms in a disinterested manner. As Freidson notes, medical professionals have a license to determine the characteristics of health and illness, and most often their judgments go unquestioned.

The evidence is clear that health and illness reflect the interests of the medical profession. Currently, various writers are speaking of a "medicalization of society" in which an increasing range of social and personal problems are defined in medical terms, while simultaneously extending the power and influence of the medical profession.[31] Thus, the idea of professional control of medical technology is both theoretically flawed and practically unrealistic. Indeed, just as the spread of technology was found to be promoted by bureaucratic strategies to control it, professionalization is also a part of this problem and not a solution.

Toward a Broader View of Controlling Medical Technology

Are all attempts to control medical technology doomed to fail? If bureaucratically imposed guidelines for using technology are ineffective and veil the broader dimensions of using medicine responsibly and if professionalization fosters vested interests rather than the needs of the patient, how can technology be checked?

A broader vision of technology must be established in order to understand its full impact on human consciousness, thus developing a medical care system that is both effective and socially responsible to the needs of patients. This entails fundamental changes in the way medical services and technology are delivered. It is not just a matter of changing the political–economic context of the health care system but, more fundamentally, the way technology and health care are conceived. The scientific status of medicine must be rethought, particularly its claim to be a positive science.

Technology has a compelling character because of the scientific assumptions on which it is predicated, particularly the mode of communication that is assumed to exist between person and machine. Nowadays this is known as instrumental communication, which eliminates "communicative competence." Communicative competence is the ability of persons to communicate the pragmatic intentions and social conditions that make behavior intelligible. Communicative competence, however, is not necessarily technological.

The medical construction of reality results from the technical communication that technology generates. It is technologically difficult to reconstruct the social conditions, biographical details, and environmental factors that give meaning to the electrochemistry of the heart, as illustrated on a screen. The ability to grasp such details—the art of medicine—is eroded with the introduction of technology because machine-produced information is not placed in the biographical–social context that makes data meaningful. Yet this artful activity is not considered scientific because it is replete with human judgments. Furthermore, it is believed that this unscientific element can be eliminated from medicine if the diagnostic process is rendered inanimate. And medicine wants to be a science.

By reifying bodily experiences, medical technology creates an image of the self as a mechanical being.[32] However, the image of one's body, following the lead of phenomenological thinkers, is central to developing human consciousness and serves as the medium for constructing the social world. A technologic image of the body—promoted by medical gadgetry and techniques—separates persons from their bodies and, therefore, deanimates the world.[33] The existential character of the body, accordingly, must be rejuvenated if technology is to be controlled.

Translating this rather philosophical point into more concrete issues, medical technology, rather than being totally discarded, must be restructured and refocused. Diagnostic techniques that obscure the biographic detail of the patient, such as automated client histories, need to be revamped to create a composite picture of the biographical details that constitute a "patient case." Beyond this, the use of nontechnology must be legitimated. This means breaking the monopoly of physicians over the health-care system. Nonscientists, those dealing in human relations, for example, need to be given power and status and their input given credence. Most generally, a holistic conception of health and illness must be institutionalized. This entails more than a call for regaining the art of medicine or establishing "free clinics" or "holistic health centers" that treat the whole person. It involves breaking with the "worldview" of scientific medicine that grips Western societies. Scientific medicine functions as a paradigm; its basic assumptions act as "incorrigible propositions" that are not testable once they are assumed. In other words, the citizenry must become iconoclastic and break the "silent assumptions" that pervade the prevailing view of health and medicine.

SUMMARY

The manner in which medical technology is currently deployed in Western societies gives cause for alarm. The gadgetry and techniques of medical science diminish health and create technologically mediated images of self and world. Because bureaucratic and professional control of technology adopts the assumptions of scientific medicine, health is defined in terms of biochemical processes. Therefore, these attempts to control technology only perpetuate a technological image of persons. This medically inspired, techno-scientific view of the social world can be changed only by de-mythologizing technology. Only in this way will medicine be in the service of humanity as opposed to instrumental reason or particular social interests. Medicine must be provided with a human base, thus enabling it to become socially responsible.

NOTES

1. Stanley Reiser, *Medicine and the Reign of Technology* (New York: Cambridge University Press, 1978).

2. George L. Engel, "The Need for a New Medical Model: A Challenge for Biomedicine," *Science* 196   (April 1977): 129–136.

3. L. Cherry, "Medical Technology: The New Revolution," *New York Times Magazine* (August 5, 1979): 12–22.

4. David Hellerstein, "Overdosing on Medical Technology," *Technology Review* 86 (August 1983): 13–17.

5. Doris Haire, "The Cultural Warping of Childbirth," in John Ehrenreich, ed., *The Cultural Crisis of Modern Medicine* (New York: Monthly Review Press, 1978), pp. 185–200.

6. Alonzo L. Plough, "Medical Technology and the Crisis of Experience: The Costs of Clinical Legitimation," *Social Science and Medicine* 15F (February 1981): 89–101.

7. K. Steel, P. M. Gertman, C. Crescenze, and J. Anderson, "Iatrogenic Illness on a General Medical Service at a University Hospital," *New England Journal of Medicine* 304 (February 1981): 638–42.

8. Ivan Illich, *Medical Nemesis: The Expropriation of Health* (New York: Bantam Books, 1977), p. 17.

9. Richard Taylor, *Medicine Out of Control: The Anatomy of a Malignant Technology* (Melbourne: Sun Books, 1979).

10. Victor R. Fuchs, "The Growing Demand for Medical Care," *New England Journal of Medicine* 279 (July 1968): 190–195.

11. Jacob M. Najman and Sol Levine, "Evaluating the Impact of Medical Care and Technologies on the Quality of Life: A Review and Critique," *Social Science and Medicine* 15F (February 1981): 107–115.

12. Reiser, *Medicine and the Reign of Technology*, p. 155.

13. Ibid., p. 158.

14. Ibid., p. 144.

15. Ibid., p. 161.

16. S. Shapiro and S. Wyman, "CAT Fever," *New England Journal of Medicine* 294, no. 17 (May 1976): 954–956.

17. Tina Posner, "Magical Elements in Orthodox Medicine," in Robert Dingwall, C. Heath, M. Reid, and M. Stacey, eds., *Health Care and Health Knowledge* (New York: Prodist, 1977), pp. 142–158.

18. Peter Conrad, "The Discovery of Hyperkinesis: Notes on the Medicalization of Deviant Behavior," *Social Problems* 23 (January 1975): 12–21.

19. Illich, *Medical Nemesis*.

20. Plough, "Medical Technology and the Crisis of Experience."

21. Robert S. Mendelsohn, *Confessions of a Medical Heretic* (Chicago: Warner Books, 1979), p. 73.

22. Barbara Ehrenreich and John Ehrenreich, *The American Health Empire: Power, Profits, and Politics* (New York: Random House, 1971), pp. 94–123.

23. Michael J. Gorun et al., "The PSRO Hospital Review System," *Medical Care* 13 (April 1975): 1–33.

24. David Mechanic, *The Growth of Bureaucratic Medicine* (New York: John Wiley, 1976), pp. 9–22.

25. This line of reasoning is developed in a provocative manner by Michel Foucault, *The Birth of the Clinic*, trans. A.M. Sheridan Smith (London: Vintage Books, 1975).

26. J. A. Skelton and J. W. Pennebaker, "The Psychology of Physical Symptoms and Sensations," in Glenn Sanders and Jerry Suls, eds., *Social Psychology of Health and Illness* (Hillsdale, N.J.: Lawrence Erlbaum, 1982), pp. 99–128.

27. For a general discussion see Jurgen Habermas, *Toward a Rational Society*, trans. Jeremy Shapiro (Boston: Beacon Press, 1970).

28. Rita Nickerson, Theodor Colton, Osler Peterson, Bernard Bloom, and Walter Hauck, "Doctors Who Perform Operations: A Study of In-Hospital Surgery in Four Diverse Geographic Areas," *New England Journal of Medicine* 295 (1976): 921–926, 982–989.

29. Talcott Parsons, "The Professions and Social Structure," in Parsons, *Essays in Sociological Theory* (New York: Free Press, 1954), pp. 34–49.

30. Eliot Freidson, *Profession of Medicine: A Study of the Sociology of Knowledge* (New York: Dodd and Mead, 1970).

31. Peter Conrad and Joseph W. Schneider, *Deviance and Medicalization: From Badness to Sickness* (St. Louis: C. V. Mosby, 1980).

32. Martin Heidegger, *The Question concerning Technology and Other Essays*, trans. William Lovitt (New York: Harper and Row, 1977).

33. See, for example, George J. Agich, "The Question of Technology in Medicine," in Stephen Skousgaard, ed., *Phenomenology and the Understanding of Human Destiny* (Washington, D.C.: University Press of America, 1981).

8

On a Critical Theory of Health Care and Social Policy: A Comparison of Habermas and Illich

John Forester

Although the work of Jurgen Habermas has received extensive attention, it has not yet been applied to the health sector.[1] This essay is a preliminary attempt both to apply Habermas's ideas to the health sector and to clarify basic health care issues.

A comparison of the work of Habermas and Ivan Illich clarifies the limits of conventional social policy and suggests a basis for future policy analysis. Illich's recent *Medical Nemesis* set off a storm of defensive criticism from medical and health professionals, but his more subtle arguments have been ignored.[2] Nevertheless, his attention to the nontechnical effects of medical care raises important questions about the use of technology, equating health care with medical care, and the role personal responsibility plays in maintaining health. Habermas treats these problems on a political, analytic, and philosophical level, while Illich provides a moral polemic. These and other differences will become clear as this comparison proceeds.

CRITICAL PERSPECTIVE: PARALLELS

Medical care may be dangerous to a person's health, Illich argues in *Medical Nemesis*. This medically induced harm, or "iatrogenesis," is clinical, social, cultural, and symbolic. Basically, he contends medical care induces pain and death, restricts personal autonomy and reactions to illness, and undermines the ability of persons to care for one another.[3] While urging a "demystification of all medical matters," Illich nevertheless writes that this deprofessionalization "does not mean the abolition of modern medicine."[4] Indeed, Illich argues that "social iatrogenesis . . . can be explained as a negative placebo, as a nocebo effect. . . . The effect of the nocebo, like that of the placebo, is largely independent of what the physician does."[5] But how can medical care be dangerous if the danger is "largely independent of what the physician does"? The answer is that a population is healthier when knowledge about health care is diffused throughout society rather than owned by a tiny minority that sells it at a price. Habermas makes a similar point when discussing public policy processes: The concentration of information distorts knowledge.

Habermas does not assess health care but the problems of legitimizing public policy. In *Toward a Rational Society*, he argues that science and technology constitute a modern, subtle ideology with far-reaching social and political consequences.[6] In *Legitimation Crisis*, he addresses the problem of achieving legitimate policies in the face of ideological distortions of ordinary communications.[7] Habermas argues that legitimate public policy is necessarily tied to domination-free discourse. Thus, he understands centralized problem solving to jeopardize the development of nonrepressive policies. Illich also understands professionalized medicine to threaten the free exchange of ideas. By outlining several similarities in their work, the merits of their criticisms can be examined.

Illich identifies the iatrogenic aspects of medicalization as: shifting responsibility for health to all-powerful medical professionals[8]; eliminating the possibilities for self-care[9]; transforming problems of health into technical issues[10]; mystifying the power of medicine and technology[11]; and distorting persons' self-image.[12] As a result, persons tend to deny the significance of personal action in health care, equate care with technology, view their existence in medical terms, and eliminate the community as a viable source of treatment.

Habermas defines "depoliticization" in ways strikingly similar to the way Illich uses the term "medicalization." A repressive society uses experts to deal with troublesome situations[13]; identifies moral matters as technical ones[14]; reduces opportunities for dialogue[15]; emphasizes social control rather than political discourse[16]; and views science and technology as central to solving social problems.[17] This means that society becomes completely rationalized, with the citizenry made to conform to a political reality that is portrayed as inviolable. Thus, alienation increases while the political status quo is reinforced.

THE PROBLEM OF TRADITION AND CONTEMPORARY APPLICATION: CAREFUL PRACTICE

Illich contends that tradition must be resurrected, for it makes social life possible as shared meanings. Illich's call is not to return to the past, but to recognize that science distorts traditional meaning.[18] Illich asks persons to recreate and regain their traditional understandings of illness, pain, suffering, or aging. Faced with the erosion of social understandings by medicalization, the positive functions of tradition must be recaptured. Still, Illich does not provide much guidance in this matter. Nevertheless, what does it mean to recreate tradition in the face of a mammoth political economy that stresses growth, efficiency, investment, specialization, and productivity?

Illich addresses, but hardly clarifies, the problem: the "alternative to a new ecological religion or ideology is based on an agreement about basic values and on procedural rules."[19] Yet the question must be asked: Whose "agreement," about which "values," and which "procedural rules"? *Medical Nemesis* suggests: "Procedures oriented to the value of survival in distribution and participatory equity are the only possible rational answers to increasing total management in the name of ecology."[20] This is not a call back to the Dark Ages, but for the recreation of tradition in a demedicalized society.

Where Illich offers little guidance, Habermas is more instructive. Habermas calls attention repeatedly to the process of communication.[21] He argues that persons should understand the disabling power of ideology as a systematic distortion of communication.[22] Dominant institutions selectively channel information, thus specifying "feasible" alternatives and giving "reasonable analyses" to social problems. Accordingly, a very limited picture of reality is offered. Habermas's call for political discourse, "will formation," democratization, and communicative activity is not a plea for information dissemination, but for the active and critical interpretation of policy problems and opportunities.[23] It is a call to reevaluate and reinterpret what policy issues really mean. Illich illuminates the myths of medicalization; that physicians are omnipotent, that medical care improves health, and that responsibility for care is equivalent to responsibility for cure. But by illustrating the sources of politically misleading communication, Habermas shows what persons need to do to demedicalize health care so that the social sources of illness are understood. His critique of distorted communications suggests what citizens must do to learn about their health, alternative modes of treatment, unrealized possibilities of caring, and the political denial of nontechnical modes of health care.[24]

A VISION OF ACTION: PRACTICAL AND COMMUNICATIVE

Habermas understands action to be not only instrumental but communicative.[25] Actions produce results and make a difference, thus being instrumental, but, additionally, they have meaning. Essentially, Habermas reformulates Max Weber's idea that social behavior is meaningful. Whereas Weber understands politically responsible action in terms of an ethic of ultimate ends or an ethic of responsibility, Habermas views political action to occur through political argument, political discourse, criticism, and dialogue, thus opening the possibilities to shape work, to critique ideology, and to make collective decisions.

Illich, by contrast, provides a more narrow vision of action that seems to be "take care of yourself." In fact, Vicente Navarro criticizes Illich for suggesting that self-care is simply "do[ing] your own thing," a call that is incompatible with collective responsibility and blind to professional power and corporate-medical interests.[26] For Habermas, true self-care requires organizing efforts so that persons can work and learn with others; collectively interpret issues, experiences, and opportunities; and make judgments and choices together about social policies.

Illich is not attentive to how communication structures and shapes information; rather, he concentrates on the problems of the isolated person.[27] Habermas's contribution, in contrast, is that he calls attention to the structural sources of personal problems and identifies "policy implications": specifically, the creation of nonalienating political communication that transforms the present structure of medicalized communications.[28] Among these changes would be publicly accountable professional review organizations, the development of transitional paraprofessional health workers, increased community-based nonmedical involvement in planning hospital care, increased incentives for health education in schools and the workplace, changes in medical education that stress the social nature of illness, and the development of community-based care facilities.[29]

Habermas addresses the issues of dependency and legitimacy much differently from Illich. For Habermas, political activity is paramount, particularly effective communication with others and the questioning of societal structures.[30] Yet because Illich's idea of action is a more personal one, the counterpoint to automony he identifies is dependency and resignation.[31] This narrow focus leads Illich to neglect the legitimacy of public policies. Illich is not overly concerned with the state or government, questions of authority or structure, or the viability of a democratic polity. Contrary to this, Habermas is concerned with the issues of legitimation and ideology and locating the crises of legitimation, meaninglessness, self-misunderstanding, and false expectations in a structural context of systematically distorted communications resulting from concentrated political-economic power.[32]

Since, for Illich, action is a matter of individual "taking care," problems of substantive state policy disappear. Because neither action nor responsibility are fundamentally political to Illich, the legitimation and justification of policies are not addressed. Illich focuses on the mystification of health care and does not examine questions related to the control of hospitals, the economic incentives that motivate physicians, the political lobbying of the American Medical Association, or other structural questions of social-political significance.[33] Attention to meaning and myth is vital, yet it should not obscure questions of political legitimacy.

TECHNOLOGY AS THE ORGANIZATION OF ATTENTION AND NEGLECT

Both Illich and Habermas are concerned with the symbolic character of technology. For them, technology is both an instrument and something that transforms society. They argue that persons act instrumentally and manipulatively, thus changing themselves as well as the world.[34] In instrumental action, technology is used to reach objectives. Nonetheless, technology fosters human aims only as long as it is democratically controlled.[35]

In other words, technology may lull persons to sleep while creating a myriad of goods. Although persons command their tools, sometimes they believe machines have power they do not really possess. For example, equating health care with medical care is a mistake, for there is a big difference between organic functioning and health.[36] Technological promises are too often understood as technological fixes, which merely delay persons from confronting the real causes of problems.[37] As Douglas Friedman points out, technology enables persons to lie to themselves, by keeping the truth about suffering, illness, and the determinants of health hidden.[38] For technology denies the symbolism, meaning, myth, and passion that are central to human existence. Yet as persons use technologies of medical care, their view of themselves begins to change. Specifically, their expectations of medicine increase as they look to science to function as religion. Medicine can produce powerful cures, but, because science is rationalistic, it is not likely that it will do much more than reduce pain. For instance, tranquilizers and other drugs are often used to quell mental anguish, grief or sorrow, and to avoid care. As technology expands it is merely cost containment, rather than the resulting human insensitivity, that concerns policy makers and the public. Thus, the logistics of technology are the focus of attention, while the social side of health care, such as good food, sewage treatment, and supportive interpersonal networks, are overlooked.

Public optimism grows as political debate is avoided concerning the accountability of physicians, the use of paraprofessionals, the public control of hospitals, and the power of medical professionals. But is pessimism avoided because political debate is eschewed? If anything, pessimism grows as medical labels are given to social problems and the power of medical professionals increases.

Lacking any democratic controls over technology, persons become dependent upon the systems established by the private sector, and forget that situations can be changed. Midwifery, for example, becomes a radical proposal, as professionals call them charlatans.[39] Health care professionals medicalize and technicize because that is what they are trained to do and they find these activities profitable and politically acceptable. As the public adapts to the resulting techniques, political and social dependency is fostered. Before this condition can be altered, the use of technology must be democratized.

Nonetheless, this is not currently the case and, as Langdon Winner notes, "reverse adaptation" is the result.[40] Ordinarily, it is thought that the problems raised by any technology relate to its control, yet a more pressing issue exists. That is, the use of technology may result in a set of unintended consequences that change the controllers as well as the "objects" controlled. Winner suggests five issues related to "reverse adaptation": Technology may affect the processes of resource exchange, result in an administrative monopoly of technical experts, begin to dictate what is socially possible in terms of what is technically feasible, create its own needs, and produce crises to justify itself.[41]

As Winner describes, rather than simply using the technology for instrumental ends, society becomes mysteriously trapped by its own creation. Moving, for example, from private to public control of medicine will not correct this situation. Additional theoretical maneuvers are necessary.

THE PRACTICE OF CRITICAL THEORY: CORRECTING SYSTEMATIC DISTORTIONS OF COMMUNICATION

Thus, Habermas and Illich call for renewed communication, criticism, and attention to the mythic, symbolic, and interpretive aspects of health care technolgies. Illich locates such communication with the ordinary person, while paying little attention to the physician's role in a demedicalized society.[42] Nonetheless, this role cannot be ignored if critical science is to delimit the proper scope of the "medical model" and to illustrate the deleterious consequences of medical symbolism for diagnosing sickness.

Health professionals shape hopes and expectations more than they produce organic changes in patients. So far, this shaping of popular consciousness has perpetuated the myth of technological salvation and the omnipotence of physicians in addition to mystifying the determinants of health. Yet Illich overlooks the responsibility of physicians for making demedicalization possible. Habermas, however, declares that experts must be publicly accountable for health care "repoliticization" or its equivalents "demedicalization" and "deprofessionalization."

Habermas claims that the doctor-patient relationship must be transformed from a technical to a dialogical one, from one of subordination to one of civil equality. Medicalization and the accompanying distortion of communication is not only a matter of belief, myth, and ideology, but also one of organization. Thus, Habermas's demand for a renewal of dialogue is not a call for increased discussion, but for political and organizational mechanisms that make open communications possible, including democratic control of health institutions, professional-community health teams, community-based care, and counseling services that empower persons to solve their own health-related problems.

Illich does not address this issue of autonomy but, in fact, writes as a classical conservative for "freedom from" external restraint and freedom to care for oneself.[43] Habermas, instead, demands freedom from domination and true political discourse.[44] Although Illich calls for the articulation of crisis and opportunity in ordinary language accessible to all,[45] it is Habermas who calls for the political institutionalization of discourse, argument, and collective "will-formation necessary for the citizenry to control health care."[46]

It is now possible to appreciate Habermas's treatment of political communication, for it is not the abstract word that acts, but rather it is persons who act as political beings. While the word has power in speech and talk can be political action, Habermas is careful to note that there is more to political argument than wordplay. True political discourse includes a critique of institutions, norms, values, and social arrangements, for without this human action may merely reinforce the prevailing system. Politics, in this sense, is critical and enlightened action. Yet to counter policy problems Illich appeals to an abstract power of tradition, while Habermas calls for political organization.[47]

While applying this political imperative to policy research, Habermas argues that there are three interests at the center of human understanding:

a.   a technical interest serving instrumental ends and constituting formal explanatory sciences;

b.   a practical interest serving interpretive and communicative ends and constituting social and historical sciences of understanding; and

c.   an emancipatory interest serving ends of liberation from unnecessary repression and toil and constituting the critical sciences.[48]

These interests suggest three different types of policy research questions:

a.   Why do persons face a given problem and what can the technical sciences do about it?

b.   What does a problem mean and how should the situation be interpreted?

c.   What should be done to thwart domination and foster collective self-determination?

Thus, Habermas is asking how policy research should be oriented in order to promote nonrepressive political organization.

    Comparing Illich's to Habermas's views on research clarifies how a proper vision of science is fundamental to sound social policies. Illich reduces science to technical problem solving and thus ignores the emancipatory potential of social science.[49] While demystifying medicine, unfortunately Illich provides little insight into the type of policy research required to demedicalize society.

    Obviously, Habermas's appeal is quite different, for he does not reduce science simply to techniques of hypothesis testing. He clarifies the relationship between technical inquiry and the practical interpretation of meaning, thus disclosing the fundamental link between science, ethics, and politics. According to Habermas, fact and value, explanation and understanding, language and world, reality and meaning cannot be separated.[50]

CONCLUSION

    A comparison of the writings of Ivan Illich and Jurgen Habermas clarifies the work that needs to be done in developing a critical theory of social policy analysis. The two authors' works are complementary as well as divergent. Both show the importance of a critique of ideology. Habermas exposes the depoliticization and legitimation of systematic distortions in communication, while Illich analyses the false expectations, self-denial, and abrogation of personal and political responsibility in a "medicalized" society. Illich points out the moral significance of the ideology of medicalization and professionalization: that is, persons' lack of autonomy and inability to care for themselves. He writes, "Compassion becomes an obsolete virtue."[51] Habermas calls attention to the structural sources of ideology and the processes whereby ideology is maintained and disseminated. Where Illich offers an admonition to develop patterns of self-care, Habermas gives organizational and structural direction on how to change health care organizations. Whereas Illich calls for a renewed appreciation of traditional modes of care, Habermas calls for democratized health care that is not simply technical, instrumental, or medical, but that is also interpretative, critical, and emancipatory.[52] Illich too narrowly equates science with technical skills, while Habermas distinguishes the two and provides technology with a human-political orientation. Illich suggests a beginning for a critical theory of health care by exposing the myths of medicalization. Habermas expands this by connecting problems of ideology to systematic distortions of communications, outlining a vision of science that is not reduced to technological inquiry, and linking problems of strategy and action to the structure of power and ownership in a capitalist political economy. Considering these differences, Habermas advanced far beyond Illich's critique of technology.

NOTES

1. Thomas McCarthy, *The Critical Theory of Jurgen Habermas* (Cambridge: M.I.T. Press, 1978); Richard J. Bernstein, *Habermas in the Restructuring of Social and Political Theory* (Philadelphia: University of Pennsylvania, 1976); Jurgen Habermas, *Toward a Rational Society*, trans. Jeremy Shapiro (Boston: Beacon Press, 1970), *Knowledge and Human Interests*, trans. Jeremy Shapiro (Boston: Beacon Press, 1968), *Theory and Practice*, trans. John Viettel (Boston: Beacon Press, 1973), *Legitimation Crisis*, trans. Thomas McCarthy (Boston: Beacon Press, 1975), and *Communication and the Evolution of Society*, trans. Thomas McCarthy (Boston: Beacon Press, 1979). See also John Forester, ed., *Critical Theory and Public Life* (Cambridge: M.I.T. Press, 1985).

2. Ivan Illich, *Medical Nemesis* (New York: Bantam Books, 1977).

3. Ibid., p. 268.

4. Ibid., p. 252

5. Ibid., p. 108.

6. Habermas, *Toward a Rational Society*.

7. Habermas, *Legitimation Crisis*.

8. Illich, *Medical Nemesis*, pp. 83, 196.

9. Ibid., p. 51.

10. Ibid., p. 37.

11. Ibid., p. 107.

12. Ibid., p. 10.

13. Habermas, *Toward a Rational Society*, pp. 102–103.

14. Habermas, *Legitimation Crisis*, pp. 86–88.

15. Habermas, *Toward a Rational Society*, pp. 102–103.

16. Habermas, *Legitimation Crisis*, p. 107.

17. Habermas, *Toward a Rational Society*, pp. 81–122.

18. Illich, *Medical Nemesis*, pp. 124, 135, 142.

19. Ibid., p. 266.

20. Ibid.

21. Habermas, *Toward a Rational Society* and *Legitimation Crisis*, Part 3.

22. Habermas, *Theory and Practice*, pp. 1–40.

23. Habermas, *Toward a Rational Society*, pp. 118–119.

24. Habermas, *Theory and Practice*, p. 12.

25. Habermas, *Toward a Rational Society*, p. 91.

26. Vicente Navarro, *Medicine under Capitalism* (New York: Neale Watson Publications, 1977).

27. Illich, *Medical Nemesis*, p. 166.

28. Habermas, *Toward a Rational Society*, pp. 118–119.

29. John Ehrenreich, *The Cultural Crisis of Modern Medicine* (New York: Monthly Review Press, 1978).

30. Habermas, *Toward a Rational Society*, pp. 81–122.

31. Illich, *Medical Nemesis*, pp. 90–91.

32. Habermas, *Legitimation Crisis*, pp. 68–90.

33. Navarro, *Medicine under Capitalism*, pp. 117–21.

34. Laurence H. Tribe, "Technology Assessment and the Fourth Discontinuity: The Limits of Instrumental Rationality," *Southern California Law Review* 46 (June 1973): 617.

35. Langdon Winner, *Autonomous Technology* (Boston: M.I.T. Press, 1976).

36. Henrik Blum, *Planning for Health* (New York: Human Sciences, 1981).

37. Illich, *Medical Nemesis*, p. 106; and John McDermett, "Technology: The Opiate of the Intellectuals," in *Technology and Man's Future* (New York: St. Martin's Press, 1977).

38. Douglas Friedman, paper prepared for Environmental Studies 137, "Resources, Environment, and Technology," Fall 1977, University of California, Santa Cruz.

39. Brian Smith-Abel, *Value for Money in Health Services* (London: Heinemann, 1976), pp. 6–7.

40. Winner, *Autonomous Technology*.

41. Ibid., p. 242.

42. Illich, *Medical Nemesis*, p. 162.

43. Ivan Illich, *Tools for Conviviality* (New York: Harper and Row, 1973).

44. Habermas, *Legitimation Crisis*, Part 3.

45. Illich, *Tools for Conviviality*, pp. 114–115.

46. Habermas, *Toward a Rational Society*, p. 69.

47. John Forester, "Questioning and Shaping Attention as Planning Strategy: Toward a Critical Theory of Planning Practice," Ph.D. Dissertation, June 1977, Department of City and Regional Planning, University of California, Berkeley.

48. Jurgen Habermas, *Knowledge and Human Interests*, trans. Jeremy Shapiro (Boston: Beacon Press, 1968), Epilogue.

49. Illich, *Medical Nemesis*, p. 162.

50. Habermas, *Knowledge and Human Interests*.

51. Illich, *Medical Nemesis*, p. 134.

52. Habermas, *Toward a Rational Society*, p. 53.

9

Politics and Technology

Joseph F. Freeman

Nowadays expressing political matters in technical terms strikes a responsive chord. Note how comforting it is to talk about politics in terms of technique. An example, overheard in a nominating caucus: "Don't tell me which one will make a good congressman! Tell me which one knows how to win elections!" Such chatter is easy to engage in, for it poses no question deeper than: "Will I like it?" today's version of "Will it work?" Campaign techniques, fifty percent of the vote plus one, constitutes the "bottom line" for our interlocutor. But this shallowness betrays an abiding weakness. In short, the ostensibly disciplined focus on technique can be, and often is, an effective foil to dealing with the full reality of a political decision, with its historical and social impact, not to mention the need for someone who can accept responsibility for events that cannot be fully controlled.

Still, technical talk is popular because there is no need to be attuned to the relatedness of events or worry about the consequences of socially complex actions. In short, the voice of political authority belongs to those who make results, who get an election to reach a preordained conclusion. Technical talk is comfortable because it is authoritative and "objective," has the ring of legitimacy, and will most likely be accepted. The bearers of such authority are worth attention and will be considered below. But most important is why people are at all disposed to accept such statements as authoritative and how in the land of the First Amendment political talk can be so circumscribed and hostile to dialogue.

TECHNOLOGY NARROWLY CONSIDERED: WORDS AND THINGS

At the outset, it must be recognized that the technical talk referred to above is also technological. A couple of pieces of evidence will serve to justify adopting the term "technology," defined as the use of science to bring about a special end. The first piece of evidence is the "junk mail" elected officials regularly receive. The letter is addressed "Dear Fellow Politico" and identifies today's successful candidates as those who use up-to-date marketing techniques. It also solicits subscriptions to a journal on campaign management that contains articles on microcomputers, software and data bases, and media strategies for polling. Also advertised are "seminars" complete with "faculties" who serve as political consultants.

The second is the promotional packet of one of the consultants featured at these seminars. It quotes a satisfied customer: "I know the pitfalls of buying without comparing the products—and I also know the confidence you have when you're using the best." "The best," however, is what appears to be a sophisticated electoral campaign software package.

The argument that valueless computers are replacing loveable politicians is not part of this essay. The only purpose of the foregoing is to establish that the ordinary talk of campaign politics increasingly employs a technologic outlook and that the persons who use the new campaign technology seem to be successful.

In one sense, this is nothing new. Any election at any period in history and in any culture will be marked by some use of whatever electoral technology is available to the campaigns. Devices in keeping with the technology of the times have always been available for influencing votes. Nonetheless, following Jacques Ellul, the question must be asked whether modern campaign technology is coming to dominate elections in ways that are quite new and forcing political action into an unbreakable technological mold.[1] Larger and more diverse electorates, progressively more complicated and expensive techniques, the vast amounts of money raised to support their use, and the effect of the technicians who must be relied upon for the proper application of these techniques raise questions about the particular relationship between technology and politics that exists today. Thus, though it seems too obvious to point out, the current technology is not just new jargon. It also encompasses complex inventions that are so intricate that only a small portion of the population can even understand them, let alone comprehend their effects.

Joan Beider has described how the application of two inventions has increased the importance of television news reporting during election campaigns.[2] The first invention is the electronic news gathering camera (ENG). Before the introduction of the ENG in the mid–1970s, sixteen-millimeter film was used to record a story. Consequently, a presidential campaign event would make the evening news only if it were over by 3:00 p.m., because time was required for film processing. Accordingly, candidates tried to do things early in the day, while announcers had to refer to events in the past tense. By contrast, when President Reagan was shot in 1981, a videotape of the event was broadcast eight minutes after the event occurred. Thus, the sense of immediacy is much sharper.

The second invention cited by Beider is the computerization of television graphics. It involves the character generator, the digital video effects machine (DVE), and their direction by computers. These also heighten the sense of immediacy in campaign and election coverage. For example, in displaying election night results on network news before 1960, the networks set up large boards with physical number panels that had to be changed manually. From 1960 to 1974, the numbers were changed mechanically. Since 1974, computer-generated graphics have been used to display numbers, letters, and backgrounds of different colors. Hence, the application of new inventions by the broadcasting networks has made campaign and election coverage more visually exciting and more immediate.

The point of this is to underscore that "technology" involves actual working inventions. In this case, it also suggests that the essential devices of contemporary political technology are inaccessible to the general public, are concentrated in a very few hands, and are devoted to heightening the illusion that television viewers are eyewitnesses to the stories presented. Similarly, direct mail technology is available only to those who have a lot of money and the expertise to conduct voter surveys.

TECHNOLOGY BROADLY CONSIDERED: RELATIONS AND CONTEXT

According to Ellul, in a technological society, "the human being is delivered helpless, in respect to life's most important and trivial affairs, to a power which is in no sense under his control."[3] A chilling observation yet, if the public is not in control, who is?

Certainly, at election time politicians do not feel that they are in control, as they sedulously court the voters' favor. Opinion polls show that the news media and intellectuals are the real controllers of society. Technological innovation, in this sense, appears to give elections their direction and meaning. Technicians determine what issues will be covered, how they will be interpreted, and the way they will be "sold" to the public. Larry Sabato has provided an insightful account of the consultants who do "scientific" polling, fund raising, and media advertising to affect the outcome of elections.[4] Accordingly, he demonstrates the inseparability of American politics and technological electioneering.

Obviously, polling is one of the most significant practices. The first political candidate to use a scientific opinion poll was Mrs. Alex Miller, a candidate for Iowa's secretary of state in 1932. The poll was conducted by her son-in-law, George Gallup, who went on to polling fame.[5] Polling is used to guide campaign strategy with remarkable precision. Tracking polls, through either simple cross-tabulations or more complex multidimensional scaling, can correlate the political opinions of respondees with their personal characteristics, and these findings allow a candidate to make direct appeals to different groups of voters. All intervening organizations are bypassed in this process as direct appeals are made to various sectors of the electorate. Thus, technological campaigning allows the establishment of a direct nexus between the candidate's campaign organization and the voter. Moreover, much of the funding for this style of campaigning comes from political action committees (PACs), which operate outside of political parties.[6] The likelihood of the political parties assuming a significant role in this type of campaign is remote. They are necessary for conducting nominations, but, as far as the electorate is concerned, parties are superfluous. With campaigns that can establish a direct link between the candidate's organization and voters, politics is no longer an activity but a state of mind.

Some find this a welcome development. If it continues, politicians will be guided by the preferences of the voters, have the means to determine their preferences, and make decisions that are supported by the public. Thus, one might conclude that a truly democratic government may be in the offing.

Clearly, this is naive oversimplification of how government actually works. Simply put, people do not have clear-cut opinions on issues and can be easily manipulated, particularly by those who are touted to be experts. Because of this, the personalities and interests of the political consultants become very important. They are not innocent bystanders, but are interested in exercising political influence on behalf of themselves. As political operatives with ambitions of exercising influence, they are unlikely candidates for membership in an "objective," Platonic ruling class. Further, they are paradoxically uninterested in the actual administration of government. As Sabato points out, these experts would rather secure the election of others to office than serve themselves:

Their substantial egos and considerable faith in their own electoral devices lead most to believe their elections would be, in the words of one, "a piece of cake." Rather, it is a dislike of actually having to serve in office, as well as a belief that merely holding a single office would mean a considerable reduction in the influence to which they have become accustomed.[7]

The excitement of election campaigns, and not legitimate governance, is their central motivation. They are gamesmen who strive intentionally to manipulate political opinions. Thus, the interlocutor at the beginning sounds less like a tough-minded, practical party operative and more like a civic voyeur, projecting his fears of personal weakness and political impotence onto a process he does not understand. For in the hands of political technicians, the polity can easily be misled into denying its real interests.

THE ATROPHY OF THE PUBLIC SELF

Thus, a thorough consideration of the technological character of politics requires more than an awareness of new inventions and who uses them. Having examined how technology is incorporated into political life, the preconceptions persons bring to politics must be analyzed. This will provide an understanding of how future technological developments will be viewed. Nonetheless, at least four centuries of literature exist that explore the relationship between technology and politics. For example, Tomaso Campanelli's *City of the Sun* and Francis Bacon's *New Atlantis*, both first published early in the seventeenth century, argue that technology could deliver society from its political follies. The popularity of B. F. Skinner's *Walden Two*, published in 1948, is evidence of the continued vitality of technological utopias. But a pessimistic rejoinder has always hounded the utopian vision. In the twentieth century technology has come, at least for the literary class, to be seen as a source of political evil rather than social reform. Specifically, technology is linked to the possibly destructive power exercised by a technological elite, yet this well-worn problem has been superseded by the suspicion that technology now obeys a dynamic of its own, divorced from the will of the polity.[8]

Early on, technology was a means to shape the future; however, this has changed. No longer is technology regarded as if it is simply a tool that can be either used or laid down at the will of the user. This is illustrated in Jacques Soustelle's remark, apropos of the French development of an atomic bomb, that "since it was possible, it was necessary."[9] To repeat, the possibilities for using new technologies cannot be separated from how persons understand themselves and their relations to others. Thus, the socially responsible use of technology may not be merely a technical issue.

Technology is driven by the principle of control. This is secured by objectifying, atomizing, and fragmenting all phenomena, including social life. Clearly, this trend is visible in American politics. Before politics can be revitalized, this trend must be reversed.

At one time, the distinctive characteristic of American politics was that large numbers of citizens were involved in the practical affairs of governance. Alexis de Tocqueville's celebration of the New England townsman, written in 1830, is the classic exposition of this viewpoint.[10] Outside the famed participatory democracy of New England as well as inside, public involvement in governmental affairs was regarded as one of the most important sources of American political strength. At the Virginia constitutional convention of 1830, reformers who wanted to have local officials elected sought the overturn of the centuries-old system of appointed county courts. Remarkably, even at this time of vigorous Jacksonian democracy, the effort failed. One of the successful defenders of the courts argued for them in terms similar to those de Tocqueville used to defend the town meeting.[11] Although the town meeting's participatory democracy differed a great deal from the county court system, apologists for each talked about them in terms of their capacity to develop citizenries with the ability to make sound judgments about practical matters of governance. This tutorial education at the local level was seen as the indispensable starting point for developing the people who would govern the United States.

Rather than summarize the complex move away from having and valuing strong institutions of local governance, it is correct to say that the process has been under way for some time. Even before World War I, American "pragmatism" rejected an openness to and sensitivity for the actual practice of governing in favor of an *a priori* commitment to a technological understanding of politics. In an essay first published in 1916, John Dewey reduced governance to purely technical terms.

With advance of knowledge, refined subtle and indirect use of force is always displacing coarse, obvious, and direct methods of applying it. This is the explanation to the ordinary feeling against the use of force. . . . It follows from what has been said that the so-called problem of "moralizing" force is in reality a problem of *intellectualizing* its use: a problem of implying so to say neural instead of gross muscular force as a means to accomplish ends.[12]

In Dewey's treatment, pragmatism did not necessarily appreciate the value and meaning of the institutions, practices, and expectations that citizens use daily to organize their affairs. Rather, government is an instrument to be used by the subtle and intelligent for ends only they understand. If Dewey is an appropriate representative of American thought, then perhaps the time is overdue for a reexamination of the national acceptance of pragmatism. At the very least, a pragmatism that neglects practice ought to be relabeled. Nonetheless, Dewey's vision of government suggests that "instrumentalism" is a more appropriate name, possibly "subjective instrumentalism."

The town meeting ultimately stagnated as an institution, never leaving New England. It was the county model of the middle Atlantic and southern colonies that was used for the framework for local government as the United States expanded westward. However, the town meeting had its revenge. It become a literary and ideological success, possibly due to de Tocqueville and his followers. Even today, the town meeting is a sentimental favorite. Yet this sentimentalism about "old-fashioned participation" effectively screens from view the profound transformation that has taken place in the practice of citizenship. To see how fully Americans have failed to come to grips with this metamorphosis, it is necessary to look beyond the political literature that still uses the vocabulary, concepts, and institutions of early nineteenth-century democracy. Most important, however, is that these changes are not epiphenomenal, but go to the heart of the American political consciousness.

One work that explores in depth the transformation of Western public consciousness is Richard Sennett's *The Fall of Public Man*.[13] A performer as well as a scholar, Sennett uses a historical account of changes in the theater and street life over the past two centuries to analyze the changes that have occurred in how people understand their relationship to society. Most germane to the present argument, he points out that for quite some time Western culture has substituted narcissism for the older conceptions of public responsibility. His explanation links the clinical definition of narcissism with the ancient Greek myth:

Narcissus kneels over a pool of water, enraptured by his own beauty reflected on the surface. People call to him to be careful, but he pays no heed to anything or anyone else. One day he bends over to caress this image, falls and drowns. . . . The myth of Narcissus has a double meaning: his self-absorption prevents knowledge about what he is and what he is not; this absorption destroys the person who is so engaged. . . . .

This is why the clinical profile of narcissism is not a state of activity, but of a state of being. . . . One drowns in the self—it is an entropic state.[14]

As should be noted, narcissism is not a psychic disorder confined to individuals, for it affects interpersonal relations and institutions as well. In conclusion, Sennett argues that social amorality reigns in the United States because life has become privatized, with everyone pursuing their own interests.

Robert Sullivan continues this theme when he declares that a "crisis of political authority develops as technology begins to dominate the domain of political and other values."[15] He brings writers such as Thomas Hobbes and the neo-Marxists of the Frankfurt school into his discussion, giving particular attention to the proposition that Marxian thought has developed a modern yet nontechnological understanding of life. Yet his readings of Jurgen

Habermas and Hannah Arendt leads Sullivan to remark that the Frankfurt school's effort to revise socialism has led to a rejection of Karl Marx, thus ending the search for "public man." Sullivan's conclusion has the same gloomy ring as Sennett's:

If the elite decides that the vast majority are incapable of transcending bodily needs, as Lenin clearly decided in "What Is To Be Done?", it follows that the elite will gain and retain power by defining politics as an activity that finally serves private ends: bread and land for the peasants, jobs and apartments for the proletarians. . . . The model need not be Soviet. It can be restated in terms of aid to Chrysler, tax cuts for the middle classes, or affirmative action programs.[16]

Sennett's and Sullivan's statements serve to illustrate how politics in America has evolved away from the democratic ideal. If the central concern of technological politics is not the creation, production, and application of inventions but instead the destruction of social relationships, then a different light is shed on both technology and how it should be used. Specifically, technology panders to the impulse of self-absorption that plagues today's society as politics becomes privatized. Thus, the belief is fostered that public policy can be guided by individualized wishes, anonymously registered on a voting machine. Moreover, technical experts are used to manipulate the fears of a polity that is fragmented. And thus it is not the content of a candidate's policies or the shared public understanding of what a candidate, once elected, might do that is important, but persons' inner feelings, taken separately, are the criteria for voting. Political technology, in this sense, transforms public life into the sum of private opinions. Yet these two factors are not at all identical.

A public engaged in dialogue is not fragmented and can formulate policies that foster the common good, as opposed to the well-being of those who are most powerful or shrewd. Furthermore, dialogue encourages persons to trust and respect one another, thereby promoting national solidarity. It is this type of togetherness that is required for Americans to solve their most pressing problems. But because technological politics obscure the collective nature of social issues, this mode of making political decisions must be abandoned. Due to the complex nature of today's problems, they can be solved only by an integrated polity.

To recognize that the technological mentality manifests itself politically does not mean that its remedy lies in politics, narrowly defined, even though political remedies must be part of an eventual cure. The depth of the matter is suggested in Sennett's reminder that narcissism is not an activity but a state of being. Because the root issue of technological politics is a matter of being, new areas of discussion must be opened that extend far beyond those usually addressed by political commentary. However, this suggestion is not entirely novel. In *The Question concerning Technology*, Martin Heidegger develops his definition of technology's essence. His prose is highly compressed, and words are used in an unfamiliar way, but it does address directly the central problem with technology. He sees technology as "the supreme danger."

This danger attests itself to us in two ways: As soon as what is unconcealed no longer concerns man even as object, but does so, rather, exclusively as standing-reserve (a stock of energy and resources), and man in the midst of objectlessness is nothing but the orderer of the standing-reserve, then he comes to the brink of a precipitous fall. . . .

In the course of seeing everything as a resource to be put to use, persons come to see things *only* in terms of how they might satisfy an individual's needs, as opposed to the common weal. "This illusion gives rise to the final delusion: it seems as though man everywhere and always encounters only himself."[17]

The salvation from this danger requires that technology neither be rejected nor embraced. Instead, reflection upon technology can lead to the recognition that it is merely a mode of understanding. Accordingly, once technology is recognized to be a style of expression it can serve human aims, instead of controlling them.

Perhaps this suggestion ought to be used to orient technological politics: Technology need not be an object of either revulsion or infatuation. Such reflection might introduce respect for daily existence and an appreciation for urbanity that is now so conspicuously lacking in political life, as well as invite persons to abandom privatism in favor of public civility.[18] Until this type of fundamental question is raised about the relationship of technology to human action, political techniques will continue to beguile the citizenry, thus destroying "public man."

CONCLUSION

A technological cast is ubiquitous to politics, particularly the actual elections. Thus, any grasp of modern elections requires attention to the technology employed. But an effective grasp of the practical consequences of technological politics requires that the fundamental predispositions of technology be examined. Hence, it is illustrated that controlling technology involves far more than merely becoming technically competent. Specifically, public life must be resurrected, so that social discourse is reinstituted as essential to politics. Nonetheless, before this can occur critical questions must be raised about technology that exceed usual political commentary. Technological rationality, simply put, must be substituted by public experience. For as long as the theoretical principles of technology go unchallenged, the world will become increasingly fragmented.

If the highest aim of statesmanship is to provide satisfaction to each citizen privately, other matters must be lower on the political agenda. Hence, Congress will not come to grips with a financial or economic policy or anything else that does not promise to stimulate individual psyches. The courts may outline guidelines concerning individual rights, but not create the public atmosphere necessary to preserve individuality. Cities will act as irresponsible corporations, thereby devaluing community life. Saddest of all, citizens will not have a practical grasp of government and politics or even know the names of their "representatives." Persons will not witness or discuss matters of state, even those closest at hand. The promotion of justice will be reserved for technical elites who invoke the fragmented technological image of society to justify their own existence. But they in turn will be governed by the whimsical preferences and appetites of a "public" free from responsibility, fraternity, or even involvement. And clearly, merely political questions, raised within such a dirempt polity, cannot change this state of affairs. Instead, public experience must be rejuvenated as a legitimate knowledge base for formulating governmental policies.

NOTES

1. Jacques Ellul, *The Technological Society*, trans. John Wilkinson (New York: Random House, 1964), p. 428.

2. Joan Beider, "Television Reporting," *Proceedings of the Academy of Political Science* 34, no. 1 (1982): 37–48.

3. Ellul, *Technological Society*, p. 107.

4. Larry Sabato, *The Rise of Political Consultants* (New York: Basic Books, 1981).

5. Charles W. Roll and Albert H. Cantril, *Polls: Their Use and Misuse in Politics* (Cabin John, Md.: Seven Locks Press, 1980), p. 10.

6. Sabato, *Political Consultants*, p. 269.

7. Ibid., p. 23.

8. Langdon Winner has refined this theme, noted above as the central one in Ellul's *Technological Society*, in Winner's *Autonomous Technology* (Cambridge: M.I.T. Press, 1977), See, for example, pp. 310–317.

9. Ellul, *Technological Society*, p. 99.

10. Alexis de Tocqueville, *Democracy in America*, vol. 1, trans. Henry Reeve, Philips Bradley, ed. (New York: Random House, 1961), p. 71.

11. *Proceedings and Debates of the Virginia State Convention of 1829–30* (Richmond: MacFarlane and Ferguson, 1854), p. 512.

12. "Force, Violence and Law," from *The New Republic*, reprinted in John Lachs and Charles E. Scott, eds., *The Human Search* (New York: Oxford University Press, 1981), pp. 40–41.

13. Richard Sennett, *The Fall of Public Man* (New York: Random House, 1974).

14. Ibid., p. 325.

15. Robert R. Sullivan, "Public Authority, Technology, Speech and Language," *Polity* 14 (Summer 1982): 585.

16. Ibid., pp. 601–602.

17. Martin Heidegger, *The Question concerning Technology and Other Essays*, trans. William Lovitt (New York: Harper and Row, 1977), pp. 26–27.

18. The possibility of civility is explored by Glenn Tinda in his *Community: Reflections on a Tragic Ideal* (Baton Rouge: Louisiana State University Press, 1980). See especially pp. 177–199.

10

Empire, Communications, and Biopower

John O'Neill

The possibilities of modern biotechnology place humans at a frontier equivalent to that where Giambattista Vico's first men found themselves.[1] Thus, the character of the human body must be rethought. This involves more than learning the new biology, as the body politic must simultaneously be reassessed because the new biology raises the spectre of a biocracy, thereby threatening democracy. In order to show the urgency of these biopolitical issues it is worthwhile to review the concepts of empire and communication in order to show how sensory and cognitive experiences have been recast. Harold Innis provides some insight into this issue inasmuch as he considers empire to be "an indication of the efficiency of communication."[2] That is to say, he believes empire and communication are inextricably related to power. Moving from Innis to Marshall McLuhan, it is possible to see that power creates a socio-text, a network or tissue of power whose external manifestation is empire. At the same time, empire organizes the *sensus communis*, shifting the ratios of experience and sensibility to rewrite the socio-text into a biotext. These issues will be clarified through an historical sketch, or genealogy, that connects the sciences of power with life.

BIOPOWER: THE BIAS OF COMMUNICATION

Innis and McLuhan contend that political history is inseparable from the history of biocommunication systems. Their works subvert the dualism in idealist and materialist historiography, because they never consider human history as anything else than an embodied history inscribed upon the *sensus communis*. History is human history, or biotextual, because it alters sensory and cognitive ratios, yet always in concert with the land, especially its rivers, forests, and minerals.[3] It is the material history of these things that under-writes the mental and sensory histories illustrated in chronicles, monuments, and laws. Yet this does not reduce communication to the techniques of information transfer. Accordingly, Innis and McLuhan reecho Vico's claim in *New Science* that persons first conceived the world with their bodies, and only later did their sensory mind yield to the scriptural mind associated with rationalism:

The human mind is naturally inclined by the senses to see itself extremely in the body, and only with great difficulty does it come to understand itself by means of reflection. This axiom gives us the universal principle of etymology in all languages: words are carried over from bodies and from the properties of bodies to signify the institutions of mind and spirit.[4]

In the light of Vico's axiom, it can be argued that the ground of universal science is the world's body, and that the world's body is the ecological setting of all other sub-rationalities. Thereby the rational sciences are grounded in poetic logic, poetic history, and poetic economy. This does not pit human reason against itself but rather bases the rational sciences in the memory of their anthro-pogenesis.[5] Thus, as Emile Durkheim and Marcel Mauss recall, all logic is grounded in the acts whereby the first humans ordered things with their familiar bodies, creating the world's first poem:

The first logical categories were social categories: the first classes were classes of men, into which things were integrated. It is because men were grouped, and thought of themselves in the form of groups, that in their ideas they grasped other things, and in the beginning the two modes of grouping were merged to the point of being indistinct. Moieties were the first genera, clans the first species. Things were thought to be integral parts of society, and it was their place in society which determined their place in nature.[6]

Initially, persons thought about society and nature with their bodies. Thus, the world was a giant body whose divisions yielded the universe, society, and nature. These imaginative universals gen-erated an embodied logic from which rationalized modes of cate-gorization were later developed. Thus, the first myths, as Claude Levi-Strauss argues, are the indispensable origin of human order and commonwealth, without which rational humanism and scientism are impossible. Vico describes the body as the basis of myth:

It is noteworthy that in all languages the greater part of the expressions relating to inanimate things are formed by metaphor from the human body and its parts and from the human senses and passions. Thus, head for top or beginning; the brow and shoulders of a hill; the eyes of needles and of potatoes; mouth for any opening; the lip of a cup or pitcher.... All of which is a consequence of our axiom that man in his ignorance makes himself the rule of the universe, for in the examples cited he has made of himself an entire world. So that, a rational metaphysics teaches that man becomes all things by understanding them (*homo intelligendo fit omnia*), this imaginative metaphysics shows that man becomes all things by not understanding them (*homo non intelligendo fit omnia*); and perhaps the latter proposition is truer than the former, for when man understands he extends his mind and takes in the things, but when he does not understand he makes the things out of himself and becomes them by transforming himself into them.[7]

Harold Innis rethinks the nature of empire and communication by assessing its development in colonial Canada, and from this deconstructs the histories of the world's great empires. Just as he sees the fate of Canada to be dependent upon the changing role of the great staples of fish, fur, timber, and wheat, so he views the history of the great empires to be related originally to communication on papyrus, clay, and stone and later books, newspapers, and radio. What is important in Innis's conception of the material history of power is that he never loses sight of the communicative struggle over knowledge or of the importance of regional resistance to communication empires that weaken democracy:

Concentration on a medium of communication implies a bias in the cultural development of the civilization concerned either towards an emphasis on space and political organization or towards an emphasis on time and religious organization.... The Byzantine empire emerged from a fusion of a bias incidental to papyrus in relation to political organization and of parchment in relation to ecclesiastical organization. The dominance of parchment in the West gave a bias towards ecclesiastical organization which led to the introduction of paper with its bias toward political organization. With printing, paper facilitated an effective development of the vernaculars and gave expression to their vitality in the growth of nationalism. The adaptability of the alphabet to large-scale machine industry became the basis of literacy, advertising and trade. The book as a specialized product of printing and, in turn, the newspaper strengthened the position of language as a basis of nationalism. In the United States the dominance of the newspaper led to large-scale development of monopolies of communication in terms of space and implied a neglect of problems of time. . . . The bias of paper towards an emphasis on space and its monopolies of knowledge has been checked by the development of a new medium, the radio. . . . The ability to develop a system of government in which the bias of communication can be checked and an appraisal of the significance of space and time can be reached remains a problem of empire and of the Western world.[8]

As will be seen later, Innis's monopolization of communicative power becomes particularly important following the appearance of biotechnology and its computerization of space and time.

McLuhan illustrates an intervening stage in this development, although his celebration of electronics is not sufficient to reconceptualize modern biopower. By way of Johann Gutenberg, the senses are restored: The eye that left its body returns as a flickering omphalos. Thus, repeating ancient symbolism, the modern house becomes a machine within a machine whose aerial (*universalis columna quasi sustinens omnia*) hooks it into the universe, floating these homes on a Milky Way of waxes, deodorants, famines, war, and inanity. Vico's poem of the world's body is now inverted—Narcissus-like—by a technology that communicates nothing but self-desire.

To behold, use or perceive any extension of ourselves in technological form is necessarily to embrace it. To listen to radio or to read the printed page is to accept these extensions of ourselves into our personal system and to undergo the "closure" or displacement of perception that follows automatically. It is this continuous embrace of our own technology in daily use that puts us in the Narcissus role of subliminal awareness and numbness in relation to these images of ourselves. By continuously embracing technologies, we relate ourselves to them as servo-mechanisms. That is why we must, to use them at all, serve these objects, these extensions of ourselves, as gods or minor religions.[9]

In the modern world, the vocabularies of public and private space and the arrangements whereby individual and collective identities are constituted are increasingly disembedded from literacy. Thus, private senses, like nationhood, have lost their closure. Indeed, following McLuhan, literacy appears only to have been a switching point in the circuitry of retribalization:

That the abstracting or opening of closed societies is the work of the phonetic alphabet, and not of any other form of writing of technology, is one theme of *The Gutenberg Galaxy*. On the other hand, that closed societies are the product of speech, drum and ear technologies, brings us at the opening of the electronic age to the sealing of the entire human family into a single global tribe. And this electronic revolution is only less confusing for men of the open societies than the revolution of phonetic literacy which stripped and streamlined the old tribal or closed societies.[10]

There is, however, an extraordinary disparity between the prophetic release of *The Gutenberg Galaxy* and his own uncritical acceptance of what might be called the McLuhanberg Galaxy. At first sight, he seems to offer a profound analysis of the structures of experience required to comprehend political power and its communicative media. In a critical comment introducing Innis's *The Bias of Communication*, McLuhan calls for the interiorization of Innis's theory of staples, which would reveal how the modern state is able to implant the circuitry of power into the human nervous system:

What Innis has failed to [do]... is to make a structural analysis of the modalities of the visual and the audible. He is merely assuming that an extension of information in space has a centralizing power regardless of the human faculty that is amplified and extended.... Visual technology creates a centre-margin pattern of organization whether by literacy or by industry and a price system. But electric technology is instant and omnipresent and creates multiple centres-without-margins. Visual technology whether by literacy or by industry creates nations as spatially uniform and homogeneous and connected. But electric technology creates not the nation but the tribe—not the superficial association of equals but the cohesive depth of the totally involved kinship groups. Visual technologies, whether based on papyrus or paper, foster fragmentation and specialism, armies and empires. Electric technology favors not the fragmentary but the integral, not the mechanical but the organic. It has not occurred to Innis that electricity is in effect an extension of the nervous system as a kind of global membrane.[11]

However, rather than pursue the biopolitical issues integral to communication, McLuhan settles for a surrealist celebration of its commercial narcosis. He fails to see that television operates as a political and commercial pacemaker implanted in the body of desire and thereby fails to wrest this medium away from the control of corporate and global capitalism. In this way, McLuhan abandons the insights he once obtained from reading newspapers and listening to the radio; namely, that the mechanical bride marries persons to the corporate economy and to its global extravaganzas. In such a marriage, political consciousness is reduced to a private and household amusement, inextricably united with the show and tell that inundates homes in the name of news and information.[12] In short, the monopoly of knowledge, as Innis calls it, which is built into the administration of the media as instruments of biopower, is obscured.

THE BIOTEXT: THE COMMUNICATIVE TISSUE OF POWER

Despite certain problems, McLuhan's thought is relevant to the new contexts of biotechnology and its consequences for the body politic. To demonstrate this, the notion of the biotext must be introduced. This means that the body is a communicative tissue upon which social power is inscribed, at first externally (the sociotext) and now in terms of the possibilities of genetic editing. If this argument is persuasive, then the distinctive contribution made by Canadian social and political thought has been outlined.

To the civilized mind, the mark of savagery is that people produce very little else than themselves. It appears that they do not alter their natural environment and are thereby committed to a minimal existence. Usually, the mark of civilization is when individuals are separated from the state, the economy, and even their families. The individual is characterized by having the power to negotiate exchanges and accumulate rights and properties that preserve a separate identity. Thus, the civilized individual is horrified by the nakedness of savages because their condition reveals that they have not separated the public and private realms. The naked savage is a social body, a sociotext. Indeed, savage societies appear to be distinct from civilized ones precisely because they embody their history by scarifying, cicatrizing, and circumcising the flesh that civilized men and women withhold from society. Civilized persons are phallocrats, for their bodies are their own, thereby providing a vehicle for personal freedom. It is only in prisons, mental hospitals, and torture chambers that modern society writes upon the flesh. As Franz Kafka puts it:

"Whatever commandment the prisoner has disobeyed is written upon his body by the Harrow. This prisoner, for instance"—the officer indicated the man—" will have written on his body: HONOR THY SUPERIORS!" ... Many questions were troubling the explorer, but at the sight of the prisoner he asked only: "Does he know his sentence?" "No," said the officer, eager to go on with his exposition, but the explorer interrupted him: "He doesn't know the sentence that has been passed on him?" "No," said the officer again, pausing as if to let the explorer elaborate his question, and then said: "There would be no point in telling him. He'll learn it on his body."[13]

McLuhan ignored the disciplinary or punitive codes that are conveyed in the media. However, once this perspective is invoked, it is possible to see all technology as biotechnology. In other words, the various historical strategies can be studied whereby the living bond between the individual and society is ritualized and thereafter continuously reproduced in various secular technologies of biopower. The first technology Jeremy Rifkin calls "pyrotechnology," which he differentiates from the new "biotechnology." Accordingly, he separates the latter into three stages, that is, genetic engineering, organism designing, and ecosystem engineering.[14] The first two will be discussed later in terms of the political economy of bioprosthetics. For the moment, it is important to see that persons' power over nature is power over themselves (as biotext), inscribed through the state, the economy, and the laws of sciences (socio-text). All of these disciplinary strategies may be thought of as biotechnologies. This move is intended as a deconstructive strategy whose aim is to bring biotechnology, as a series of specific biological and medical engineering practices, within the realm of biopolitics. Hence, it is important to note that modern societies are devising technologies for rewriting the genetic code, much as savage societies once rewrote the flesh in order to alter the body of desire. Alphonso Lingis describes this in the following manner:

For capitalism is the state in which all the excitations, all the pleasures and pains produced on the surface of life are inscribed, recorded, fixed, coded on the transcendent body of capital. Every pain costs something, every girl at the bar, every day off, every hangover, every pregnancy, and every pleasure is worth something. The abstract and universal body of capital fixes and codes every excitation. They are no longer, as in the bush, inscribed on the bare surface of the earth. Each subjective moment takes place as a momentary and singular pleasure and pain recorded on the vast body of capital circulating its inner fluxes . . . in short, there is . . . a going beyond the primary process libido to the organization man. The dissolute, disintegrated savage condition, with the perverse and monstrous extension of an erotegenic surface, pursuing its surface affects, over a closed land inert, sterile body without organs, one with the earth itself—this condition is overcome, by the emergence of, the dominion of, the natural and the functional. The same body, the working body, free, sovereign, poised, whose proportion, equilibrium and ease are such that it dominates the landscape and commands itself at each moment. Mercury, Juno, Olympic ideal.[15]

The biotechnical history of the modern body is only now emerging. It involves a simultaneous rewriting of the history of the human sciences. This is difficult to understand because social scientists are unaccustomed to dealing with the embodied subject whose life is wagered in their enterprise.[16] Most important at this juncture is the historical convergence of medical discourse and the vocabularies of state and economic power, which operate on the new frontier of biotechnology. The aim is to deconstruct the preconceptions of political economy that rule the physical body either by force or by the transformation of private desires into public needs. The constraints imposed by society and the state, when they are enforced externally, require torturous discipline to inscribe in the mind of the public the law's imperious nature. A decisive shift occurs once the state finds a medium of communication that enables it to exploit the connection between minds and bodies more directly than in its early theatre of cruelty. This shift occurs, as Michel Foucault argues, when the modern state discovers that knowledge can be used to rewrite the socio-text, thus extending biopower to every facet of individual and collective life:

To analyse the political investment of the body and *the microphysics of power* presupposes, therefore, that one abandons—where power is concerned—

the violence-ideology opposition, the metaphor of property, the model of the contract of conquest . . . one might imagine a political "anatomy." . . . One would be concerned with the *"body politic,"* as a set of material elements and techniques that serve as weapons, relays, *communication routes and supports for the power and knowledge relations that invest human bodies and subjugate them by turning them into objects of knowledge.*[17]

Here, too, is found a history from Innis, through McLuhan to Foucault, which describes an *archeology of power.* Essentially, the state's territorial inscription (the socio-text), along with its theater of cruelty, is changed because of the discovery that the production of human knowledge, desire, intelligence, health, sexuality, and sanity can be accomplished by a communicative network of biopower inscribed within the body, binding every body into a new Leviathan, or biotext. Obviously, this history cannot be told in all of its detail by any single historian or social scientist, and this discussion provides only a preliminary conceptual analysis of this issue. Nonetheless, the modern state is now concerned to legislate the origins and ends of life and to terminate life with more intensive strategies than feudal and absolute monarchies could muster. Of course, modern states also exercise power in foreign affairs as a major component of the economy. These strategies of power are not always congruent. In liberal democracies, state power simultaneously defends and undermines the mental and bodily integrity of its subjects.[18] At its lowest points, the state now practices forms of torture equal to the horror of Kafka's penal colony. In its seemingly benign form, the modern state, like the corporate economy, seeks to control minds and cajole behavioral desire rather than to command it with the ultimate sanction of bioforce. In practice, the state and the economy move between these two extremes. Increasingly, however, the therapeutic state enforces conformity through persons' desire for health, education, and employment, not to mention happiness.[19] This is what is meant when it is suggested that all technologies are biotechnologies and that in turn they are strategies of biopower.

Everyone wants to avoid genetic damage and counteract infertility or dangerous births. These motives are at first humane. Yet the technologies for promoting these goals may be inhumane. Indeed, there is already enormous concern and considerable legislative activity on this score, yet the present focus must be on how the basic metaphors of communications serve to extend biocracy. Although the aim is not to exaggerate the implications of biogenetics for politics, nevertheless, a double claim is entered in the debate on genetic engineering.[20] The first, of course, is the technological *a priori*, that is, "if it can be done, it must be done." There is, however, a second claim, namely, that "in science, of course, what is impossible now, may well be possible later." Thus, the only solid objection to the technological *a priori* is, "even if it can be done, it should not be." Here, however, science, and not only the life sciences, is likely to be invoked to settle this issue. This view is likely to prevail because DNA, as the fundamental component of life and communication, is conceived to dominate all other discursive codes and control existence.[21]

Biotechnology must be seen in terms of two prosthetic strategies, one now largely available and the other increasingly possible: spare part prosthetics and genetic prosthetics. These two strategies are available for rewriting the biotext, thereby equating "spare part" persons with those who are capable of self-actualization.

In the mechanist vision each organ is still only a partial and differentiated prosthesis: a "traditional" simulation. In the bio-cybernetic view it is the smallest undifferentiated element, it is each tiny cell that becomes an embryonic prosthesis of the body. It is the formula inscribed in each tiny cell that becomes the true modern prosthesis of all bodies. For if the prosthesis is ordinarily an artifact which supplants a failing organ, or the instrumental extension of a body, then the DNA molecule, which contains all the relevant information belonging to a living creature, is the prosthesis par excellence since it is going to permit the indefinite prolongation of this living being by himself—he being nothing more than the indefinite series of his cybernetic vicissitudes.[22]

The two strategies, although seemingly on the same biomedical frontier, are in fact very different. That is to say, the economy of spare part prosthetics involves a combination of medical craft, commercial banking, and distribution procedures. These systems may be entrepreneurially or state managed and may draw upon voluntary donors. Yet, as Richard Titmuss shows in the case of blood supply, there are a number of problems with quality and continuity in the supply of spare part prosthetics.[23] These problems could be circumvented, however, if it were possible to anticipate genetic faults and to correct them at the DNA level. Indeed, to the extent that genetic engineering is possible, market rationality and efficiency may be implanted at the DNA level. Simply put, biologically perfect embryos could be a matter of parental choice. A mark of such perfection, from the point of view of the parent, might consist of cloning embryos. If that were indeed a possibility, then biotechnology would finally deliver the myth of Narcissus. Biotechnology would deanimate the body and the imagination of pure individuals by making them the product of the dominate ethos of either the market or the state. Under such conditions the institution of life is radically altered. For example, religious and political institutions, such as the Bible and parliament, would cease to be fundamental. For in the laboratory or the clinic, life no longer has any history. Birth becomes a consumer fiction like Mother's Day and thereafter embodied family histories float in a commercial narcosis monopolized by an entrepreneurial and a statist biocracy, thus realizing the nightmare of 1984.

Genetic engineering is enchanting because it reanimates the myth of prosthetic man.[24] This activity is all the more engaging since it appears that the biotext, needed for this refurbished myth, is encoded in the basic material of life. Although he dismisses much of the science surrounding genetic engineering, P.B. Medawar's formulation of the historical and demographic implications of biotechnology echoes the utopian dream of the administrative state devised by Plato in *The Republic*:

At the root of all genetic engineering lies . . . the greatest scientific discovery of the twentieth century: that the chemical make-up of the compound deoxyribonucleic acid (DNA)—and in particular the order in which the four different nucleotides out of which it is assembled lie along the backbone of the molecule—encodes genetic information and is the material vehicle of the instructions by which one generation of organisms governs the development of the next. If the DNA message is altered, the effects of doing so are, in their context and of their kind, as far reaching as the effects would be of altering the wording of congressional or parliamentary legislation or the wording of telegrams conveying diplomatic exchanges between nations.[25]

Even though Medawar dismisses the wildest variations of biocracy, he, Rifkin, and Gerald Leach consider that a fundamental constitutional change is imminent, as the basic character of life is being rewritten. Most problematic, however, is that this process is being directed from an extra-political site. This is because the confines of the laboratory are ahistorical. Biopolitics, in this sense, makes political life apolitical since human interaction is substituted by genetic manipulation.

NOTES

1. John O'Neill, "On the History of the Human Senses in Vico and Marx," in O'Neill, *For Marx against Althusser*, (Washington, D.C.: University Press of America, 1983), pp. 81–87.

2. Harold A. Innis, *Empire and Communications*, revised by Mary Q. Innis (Toronto: University of Toronto Press), p. 9.

3. John O'Neill, "Facts, Myths and the Nationalist Platitude," *Canadian Journal of Sociology* 1, no. 1 (1975): 107–124.

4. Giambattista Vico, *The New Science of Giambattista Vico*, translated from the 3d edition by Thomas Goddard Bergin and Max Harold Fisch (Ithaca and London: Cornell University Press, 1970), pars. 126–127.

5. John O'Neill, *Five Bodies: Studies in Radical Anthropomorphism* (Ithaca, N.Y.: Cornell University Press, 1985).

6. Emile Durkheim and Marcel Mauss, *Primitive Classification*, Rodney Needham, trans. and ed. (London: Cohen and West, 1963), pp. 82–83.

7. Vico, *The New Science*, par. 405.

8. Innis, *Empire and Communication*, p. 170.

9. Marshall McLuhan, *Understanding Media: The Extensions of Man* (New York: McGraw Hill, 1965), p. 46.

10. Marshall McLuhan, *The Gutenberg Galaxy: The Making of Typographic Man* (Toronto: University of Toronto Press, 1962), p. 8.

11. Marshall McLuhan, "Introduction," in Harold A. Innis, *The Bias of Communication* (Toronto: University of Toronto Press, 1951), p. xiii.

12. John O'Neill, "McLuhan's Loss of Innis-Sense," *The Canadian Forum* 41, no. 709 (May 1981): 13–15.

13. Franz Kafka, "In the Penal Colony," in Nahum N. Glatzer, ed. *The Complete Stories*, (New York: Schocken Books, 1971), pp. 144–145.

14. Jeremy Rifkin, *Algeny: A New Word* (New York: Penguin Books, 1983), p. 215.

15. Alphonso F. Lingis, "Savages," *Semiotexte* 3, no. 2 (1978): 101–102.

16. John O'Neill, *Sociology as a Skin Trade: Essays towards a Reflexive Sociology* (London: Heinemann, 1972).

17. Michel Foucault, *Discipline and Punish: The Birth of the Prison*, trans. Alan Sheridan (New York: Vintage Books, 1979), p. 28 (emphasis added).

18. John O'Neill, "Defamilization and the Feminization of Law in Early and Late Capitalism," *The International Journal of Law and Psychiatry* 5 (August 1982): 255–269.

19. John O'Neill, "Looking into the Media: Revelation and Subversion," in Michael A. Hyde, ed., *Communication Philosophy and the Technological Age* (University: University of Alabama Press, 1982), pp. 73–97.

20. June Goodfield, *Playing God: Genetic Engineering and the Manipulation of Life* (London: Hutchinson and Co., 1977).

21. Gerald Leach, *The Biocrats: Implications of Medical Progress* (London: Penguin Books, 1972), pp. 153–154. For the use of other communications metaphors, such as blue print, punch card, genetic alphabet, genetic dictionary, universal language of life, see Edward Frankel, *DNA: The Ladder of Life* (New York: McGraw-Hill, 1979), Ch. 7, "DNA and the Genetic Code of Life."

22. Jean Baudrillard, *De la seduction* (Paris: Editions galilee, 1979), pp. 231–232.

23. Richard M. Titmuss, *The Gift Relationship: From Human Blood to Social Policy* (New York: Vintage Books, 1971).

24. Sigmund Freud, *Civilization and Its Discontents*, trans. and ed. James Strachey, (New York: W. W. Norton and Company, 1962), pp. 38–39.

25. P. B. Medawar, "Fear and DNA," *The New York Review of Books* (October 27, 1977): p.15.

11

Technological Consciousness and Education

John R. Scudder, Jr.

The impact of technology on learning is evident in the way persons nowadays talk about education. Schools are "plants" and students their "most important products," as production is measured by quantifiable behavioral objectives. Teachers who "increase production" are given "merit" pay, while students are treated as raw material. Accordingly, teachers use "positive reinforcement" to shape their students' behavior.

In this technological view of education neither teachers nor students are regarded as persons. Teachers are regarded as components of a system who must meet certain competency criteria specified for certification, such as the standards specified by the National Teachers Examination. When "experts" in personnel management determine they have met the requisite standards, teachers are "plugged into" the education system in the appropriate place. Students, too, are regarded as raw material, although they are called "individuals." Individual needs and interests, however, are taken into account only in terms of making a satisfactory product. Accordingly, the needs of children are "assessed" by experts in behavioral science so that the most effective educational methods are adopted. Regardless of whether education is viewed as "child centered" or society centered, both teachers and students are objects of production, which is articulated in the language of technology.

A CRITIQUE OF POPULAR TECHNOLOGICAL CONSCIOUSNESS

Yet when most people think of technology they do not think of consciousness but merely of technological devices. The latest technological device that is supposed to revolutionize education is the computer. Most educators and parents view this device as merely an effective means of instruction and thus fail to recognize that it alters the consciousness of students. Recently, five criticisms of the technological consciousness that accompanies the use of computers in the classroom have been noted.[1]

First, the learning progress is fragmented because experience is serialized. Although these devices supposedly "individualize" learning, in fact they do the opposite. Because students learn by following a step-by-step predetermined logic, learning is completely controlled. Hence, when parents try to help their children by suggesting alternate ways of solving a math problem, their children are completely confused. This is because their children have been taught *the* way by the machine. Students are presented with absolute knowledge and thus do not learn that information needs to be interpreted, challenged, expanded, and related to the everyday world.

Second, technological learning reduces teaching to monological discourse. Information proceeds from a sender to a receiver without the receiver understanding that messages come from other human beings and have a history. Students are given "predigested" categories to be "mastered," into which data are neatly placed. Thought is thus associated with machine logic and not interpersonal dialogue.

Third, technological education requires and fosters instrumental learning. The goal of this style of learning is efficiency, which requires quick response, the rapid assimilation of information, and the expeditious movement from premises to conclusions. A child can be "handicapped" by being a thoughtful reader with a poetic love of language because technological learning rewards those who rapidly process information and penalizes those who think creatively.

Fourth, technological educators stress the manipulation of information, otherwise known as problem solving. Problem solving here is not innovation but exercises that seek immediate results. Thus, students are not encouraged to reflect on situations and to explore the ambiguities involved in solving problems but merely to apply predigested knowledge uncritically.

Finally, technological pedagogy assumes that humans are passive, amoral receivers and appliers of information. Students are conditioned to receive laws, logic, and techniques that are applied in prescribed ways without any concern for creativity. In sum, students are regarded as raw material to be formed into products and not as persons who interact with others while shaping the world.

THE PHILOSOPHICAL FOUNDATIONS OF TECHNOLOGICAL CONSCIOUSNESS IN EDUCATION

John Dewey laid the foundations for contemporary technological consciousness in education and probably he would be appalled at the popular "offspring" of his philosophy. In fact, John Murphy and John Pardeck contend that modern technological education "is not the activistic style of practice advocated by John Dewey, which requires that personal or pragmatic motives serve to determine the utility of knowledge."[2] This, of course, is true. Nonetheless, Dewey's instrumentalism is based on a technological view of education. The root of Dewey's technological consciousness of education is Charles Darwin's model of evolution. Having taken his basic model from the study of nature rather than human beings, Dewey inadvertently adopts a technological approach to education.

Because Dewey's conception of human beings originates with the evolutionary model, he regards persons as basically active, with their activity guided by habits. When these ways fail to bring about satisfactory adjustment to the environment, problems arise. Accordingly, he cites a series of steps that are followed when remedying these difficulties. First, the mind senses the problem. Second, it defines the problem. Third, it develops hypothetical solutions to the problem. Fourth, it selects the hypothetical solution most likely to solve the problem. Finally, it applies the solution. In short, the mind's main function is problem solving, adopting what Dewey refers to as the scientific method. Thus, human freedom results from using the mind to solve problems. Yet is Dewey's view of freedom self-direction? For it must be remembered that human growth depends on the ability to make value judgments, to see opportunities for realizing these values, and to take action to bring about their realization.[3]

Dewey applies his instrumental philosophy to education. For him, a curriculum is a sequence of experiences that maximizes future growth and interaction with the socio-cultural environment. Central to this process is problem solving. Because Dewey believes that problem solving is integral to learning, he regards the teacher as a guide who helps students interact effectively with their environment. Education for Dewey, unlike the progressives, goes beyond meeting the needs and interests of students by stressing rational self-direction through the mastery of scientific inquiry.[4]

Although Dewey claims to be applying the scientific method to education, actually he makes education into high-level technology. As Isaac Berkson points out, Dewey neglects the theoretical, conceptual, and mathematical bases of science but rather views science as simply an operational procedure.[5] This led him to confuse science with technology. He did not teach educators to think scientifically about education but technologically, or "instrumentally." That the instrumental is technological, rather than scientific, is made very clear by Martin Heidegger.[6] Heidegger recognizes the danger in a Deweyan instrumentalism when he points out that the "coming to presence of technology threatens revealing, threatens it with the possibility that all revealing will be consumed in ordering."[7] In other words, technological consciousness may come to stifle human action or creativity. Had Dewey claimed that instrumentalism was one way of articulating education, his philosophy of education would be difficult to criticize. However, he claims that instrumentalism is the only adequate approach to education.[8] Accordingly, it is possible to show the limitations of the technological approach to education by demonstrating how his instrumentalism distorts this process.

INTEGRAL CONSCIOUSNESS AND EDUCATION

Dewey believes that education must be integrated into the everyday life of students. He contends that academic subjects that divorce education from the problems faced by students prevent them from achieving an integral consciousness. Unfortunately, Dewey fails to delineate an adequate model of integrated consciousness because he regards students as merely organisms that interact with an environment. By treating students as objects rather than subjects, they are blinded to the meaning of lived time and the way language constructs the social world.

There are at least five major obstacles to helping students achieve an integrated consciousness. The first concerns integrating a curriculum that consists of many distinct subjects. The second pertains to overcoming the social fragmentation imposed by clock time. The third concerns integrating students of different backgrounds without suppressing them with the demands made by the dominant culture. The fourth relates to integrating persons' educational experiences without objectifying students. And the fifth relates to making students aware of the nexus of human action and world.

Academic Disintegration and Instrumental Reduction

The divisive effect of a curriculum on consciousness has been a central concern for American educators. Yet most have attempted to resolve this issue by merely manipulating the curriculum, by reorganizing subjects into broad fields such as humanities, social studies, and natural sciences. Rather than integrating a student's consciousness, this approach divides it in ways that are culturally unfamiliar.

The fundamental problem with the broad fields approach is that it is based on the principle of misplaced concreteness, as identified by Alfred North Whitehead. It assumes that the subjects are concrete and, therefore, the solution of the problem of integral consciousness is to combine them. Edmund Husserl shows, however, that the life world and not academic subjects constitutes a person's experiences.[9] Accordingly, he suggests that theoretical disciplines should be organized with reference to the life world. For example, adequate instruction in botany requires an examination of the trees encountered in everyday experience. A tree may be studied as an example of photosynthesis, esthetically as beautiful form, or practically as potential board feet of lumber. Yet the tree is not three different trees because it is examined from three different perspectives. In short, the problem of fragmenting consciousness by dividing a curriculum is not solved by creating broader subjects, but by helping students to see that theoretical studies enable them to understand the life world of their daily experience in different ways. In this way, a curriculum is integrated through experience.

Dewey understood that when subjects are taught as ends in themselves students are artificially separated from their everyday experience.[10] He contends that education should treat the problems students actually face daily, and that a curriculum should be organized around these issues. Dewey believes that problem solving is a solution to consciousness being divided by subjects and to the separation of the school experiences from everyday life. Nonetheless, he fails to see that his rigid technological method blinds students to all aspects of the world that cannot be articulated and explained instrumentally. In addition, it reduces students to complex adaptive organisms, thereby denying that they are subjects who engage the world in many ways. In short, Dewey does not grasp the need for persons to think theoretically, as opposed to just instrumentally.

Lived Time and Clock Time

Dewey's problem-solving approach to education seems to favor lived time over clock time for organizing educational experience, for he rejects the traditional notion that subjects should be offered at specific times. Accordingly, students are to order their time in accordance with the problem to be solved. This approach to time is somewhat similar to that of the Montessori school described by Valerie Suransky.[11] In this school, time is ordered by the individual project to be completed, as opposed to the "typical" kindergarten where there is "take off your coat time," "play time," "orange juice and cookies time," and so forth.

Yet in neither the clock time school nor the Montessori school is time "lived time." Suransky demonstrates this while studying an inner-city black kindergarten, in which schedules are flexible and subject to change. Activities are not organized around the "linear" task time of the step-by-step methodology prescribed by Montessori and Dewey. Instead, projects are chosen and carried out individually and collectively. Rather than adapting to the environment through a linear and scientific progression of events, these students see possibilities in their current situation that they transform into future activities. Thus, their time is lived time rather than clock or linear task time, as the future is created out of the present. This time is lived by each student and not prescribed by someone else as in traditional education. Accordingly, a student's day is organized around task experience, as opposed to a set of tasks that are scheduled to be completed.

Integrating the Culturally Different into the Common Culture

Living one's own time does not imply living alone, however, for the idea of society implies the existence of a common culture. Most often, schools are thought to instill these values. The actual organization of schools, nonetheless, raises the issue of how the culturally different can achieve full enculturation and at the same time live and learn authentically. Many educators articulate this issue in terms of a struggle of rights. For example, conservative educators ask, "What right do blacks have to demand changes in the traditional education system?" Liberal educators, on the other hand, ask, "What right does the dominant culture have to force its views on a minority?" This struggle of rights is fostered by Dewey since culture is understood as an external environment.

In contrast to Dewey, Remy Kwant, like most phenomenologists, understands culture as a way of being in the world, or a socially constructed reality. Thus, enculturation is initiation into the lived world of adults, as certain systems of meaning and acting are required to live well as an adult.[12] Culturally disadvantaged persons, then, are those whose enculturation has not prepared them to live within the system of meanings considered valid by a given society and thus have limited possibilities for self-expression and for making a positive contribution to the commonweal.

A culturally different student has adequate systems of meanings and values for living with his or her reference group. However, these meanings and values are insufficient for a student to function adequately in the broader society. Yet integration into a new society does not necessarily require that persons sacrifice their identity to the dominant culture. When a black is required to become an "Uncle Tom" to succeed in school, this is not cultural integration.

This problem could be resolved by persons' demanding rights if they were objects with fixed needs and interests. But human beings are subjects who become what they are through interaction with other human beings. Accordingly, many black children are both culturally disadvantaged and culturally different. Yet when educators only aim at overcoming their disadvantages, students are prevented from expressing themselves. On the other hand, if teachers attempt only to cultivate students' cultural differences, students become alienated from the broader society. Technological education, however, does not recognize this difference, as all students are made to conform to one style of instrumental thinking. As such, students must abandon their individuality as part of the learning process. Contrary to this technological viewpoint, promulgated by Dewey, students must be shown that order can emerge out of the *recognition of difference*. Yet before this can be appreciated, the type of objectification advocated by technology, which treats students as irrational and incapable of interacting with each other, must be rejected. Only in this way will individualism and order be able to coexist, for otherwise it will be thought that society is possible only if everyone bases their actions on an identical body of knowledge.

Integral Consciousness and Languages

Another issue related to integrating consciousness and education is the reduction of human experience through the use of propositional language. For, as Dewey contends, problem solving requires propositional language, the language of science and technology. However, developing an integral consciousness requires the use of all the dimensions of language: evocative and expressive as well as propositional.

Most educators, like Dewey, stress only the propositional dimension of language, as students are instructed to arrange the world in linear manner, to focus on things, and to relate ideas to things. In short, students are taught to be analytical rather than synthetic. This means that they make statements about that world, are taught to see it "as it is" and not as it ought to be, and regard the world as a sum of parts not as a whole.

However, children come to school with evocative and expressive modes of language and are moved by symbolic expressions. They express their feelings about their world spontaneously and act creatively. Rather than enhancing and cultivating these "natural" ways of relating to the world, they are told that propositional language is the only legitimate language. By the time students reach high school, they can discuss analytically the structure of a poem but they have lost all poetic expression. They can discuss the structure of government but have little commitment to good citizenship or public service. Thus, they lose their capacity for living in the evocative and expressive language that is central to the world.

The expressive dimension of language, as interpreted by Maurice Merleau-Ponty and others, embodies the lived world. Thus, for example, good teachers of physics teach in the expressive dimension of language even when explaining physics in propositional terms. They evoke enthusiasm for the pursuit of truth and show the contributions physics has made to society. They focus their theories on the lived world so that what is opaque to everyday consciousness becomes evident to students. Unfortunately, many physics teachers do not stress the various dimensions of language for, after all, propositional language is the language of physics. Nonetheless, propositional language should not be the only language for articulating knowledge and experience. For example, literature teachers who teach students to analyze the plot of *Hamlet*, without helping them to appreciate how it is actually performed, prevent students from experiencing art. In addition, when students do not grasp the human dilemma that is faced by Hamlet, they miss the relationship of art to life. History teachers who factually describe and analyze the battles of the Revolutionary War, without expressing the petty jealousies, fears, and frustrations that George Washington encountered, distort history. In short, the humanities must be taught in all dimensions of language if human experiences are to be revealed. In fact, all subjects should recognize the multivalent nature of language, for only in this way are human experiences viewed as central to education and the world implicated in expression.

THE PERSONAL CONTEXT

Science itself makes sense only within a personal context, that is, as an activity engaged in by persons who seek to understand the world. Additionally, the educational process is intelligible only within a personal context. Yet Dewey places education within a naturalistic, as opposed to a human context. In fact, Dewey goes so far as to argue that the human organism should be called "it."[13] This is a classical example of the naturalistic reduction of human beings to things. Things, unlike humans, do not relate to their environment through systems of meaning. Dewey's naturalistic model, accordingly, does not emphasize human meaning.

Yet education initiates the young into the world through reappropriating human systems of meaning developed originally by other persons. Further, children are introduced to the world by persons who relate to the world through these systems of meaning. Thus, it seems that education should be allied with the human sciences and their methods. However, Dewey regards the procedures scientists use for understanding and controlling the natural world as appropriate for directing personal growth, as all human relationships are subsumed under the problem-solving method.

Actually, Dewey has the cart before the horse, since human beings understand problems in terms of their interpersonal relationships. For example, marriage partners may have a problem relative to them living together. But their marriage is not constituted by problems. Rather, they face and attempt to resolve their problems within the interpersonal context of marriage. Therefore, the way to understand their relationship is to view it as interpersonally constituted. Human beings do not simply adapt to the environment by problem solving but create problems through their encounters with other people. Persons, in short, establish the context within which problems exist.

Also, education is constituted by persons helping others to recognize and realize their possibilities in the world. During this process, teachers initiate other persons who are less enculturated into the systems of meaning, valuing, and acting of their culture. In a democratic society, this is done in a way that promotes critical self-direction. Clearly, education occurs within a personal context rather than a natural or technological one.

The personal context of education is lost when education is limited to technological consciousness. In fact, students become problems, rather than persons with whom teachers relate as fellow human beings. In technological renditions of special education this is evident. Children become "special" by being categorized as mentally retarded, emotionally disturbed, or learning disabled. Teachers are taught to deal with these problems by experts in the behavioral sciences. From them, teachers learn technological methods for altering the behavior of their "special" students so that they can better adapt to their environment. In order to bring about this behavior, teachers establish behavioral objectives that their students have to achieve. When students achieve these objectives they are rewarded, thereby reinforcing their new behavior.

In contrast, consider a teacher in special education who understands his or her students to be special, not by categorization, but because they are unique. Of course, the teacher understands the behavioral problems of the children and is adept in using operant conditioning. Moreover, the teacher establishes behavioral objectives and the students usually achieve them. But when the teacher talks about the students, they are particular persons, not examples of certain types of disabilities. For instance, the teacher talks about John Smith and of the "neat" way he does this or that and exhibits real concern about his difficulties. When asked for the causes of this child's problems, the teacher gives an expert analysis of his limitations and of the ways experts suggest they should be treated. Yet when the teacher uses these expert prescriptions, he or she does so in ways that are a part of a personal relationship with this particular child. The teacher does not relate to students as an expert who solves physical or mental problems by technological means.

Technological consciousness has an important place in education. It can help teachers teach more effectively and help students learn how to relate to the world instrumentally. But when it becomes the way of structuring consciousness, students and teachers are channeled into one way of experiencing life, which limits and distorts their relationships to the world and each other. Thus, technological consciousness inhibits rather than fosters integral consciousness. Further, it treats people like things to be controlled and shaped by others. However, technology can contribute to human freedom, as Dewey believes. But it can do this only by being placed in a personal context, rather than a natural one. Following this, it becomes one means of freeing persons from natural and behavioral limitations, so that they can realize their possibilities, become self-directing, and establish fulfilling interpersonal relationships.

NOTES

1. John W. Murphy and John T. Pardeck, "The Philosophical Underpinnings of Technological Education," unpublished paper, Arkansas State University, 1984, pp. 6–12.

2. Ibid., p. 10.

3. Dewey did, of course, devote much attention to the process of making value judgments, but John Smith has shown why Dewey could not treat values adequately within his instrumental philosophy. See John E. Smith, *The Spirit of American Philosophy* (Oxford: Oxford University Press, 1963), pp. 139–158.

4. John Dewey, *Experience and Education* (New York: Collier Books, 1963), pp. 33–50, 61–67, 73–88.

5. Isaac B. Berkson, "Science, Ethics, and Education in the Deweyan Experimentalist Philosophy," *School and Society* 87 (October 10, 1959): 387–388.

6. Martin Heidegger, *The Question Concerning Technology and Other Essays*, trans. William Lovitt (New York: Harper and Row, 1977), p. 5.

7. Ibid., p. 33.

8. Dewey, *Experience and Education*, p. 88.

9. Edmund Husserl, *Phenomenology and the Crisis of Philosophy*, trans. Quentin Lauer (New York: Harper Torchbooks, 1965), pp. 149–192.

10. Dewey, *Experience and Education*, p. 78.

11. Valerie Polakaw Suransky, *The Erosion of Childhood* (Chicago: University of Chicago Press, 1982), pp. 59–66; 79–106, 136–142.

12. Remy C. Kwant, *Phenomenology of Social Existence*, (Pittsburgh: Duquesne University Press, 1965), p. 78.

13. John Dewey, *Experience and Nature* (New York: Dover Publications, 1958), p. 232.

12

Toward a Justification of Rhetoric as Technique

David Descutner and DeLysa Burnier

Examining the effects of technology upon society and culture has long preoccupied both continental and American scholars. Karl Marx, Thorstein Veblen, Max Weber, W. F. Ogburn, Jacques Ellul, and Lewis Mumford, among many others, have all explored questions linked to the impact of technology. The purpose here is not to review the history of the study of technology, but rather to inquire into certain questions that these studies address only indirectly. Specifically, this chapter will address the manifold relations among technique, language, and knowledge.

Agreeing with Paul de Man that the "paradigmatic structure of language is rhetorical," modern writers argue that rhetoric is a form of technique that bears fundamentally on human understanding and the use of language, knowledge, and truth.[1] This rhetorical perspective upholds the significance of interpretation without resorting to the hermetic arena of poststructuralism, from which the life world of experience is excluded. Accordingly, as opposed to poststructuralism, this discussion rehabilitates the political dimension of interpretation by reinvesting language with the animating force of political experience. Indeed, it is precisely the absence of this force that renders barren the poststructuralist accounts of the "tropics of discourse."[2] Ultimately, the aim here is to justify rhetoric as a technique that constitutes knowledge and truth and offers the possibility of freedom through critique and reform.

To accomplish this, the competing views of rhetoric as technique that originated in the debate between the sophists and Plato are presented. With this classical debate between sophistic rhetoric and Platonic philosophy as a touchstone, the modern period where Marx and Friedrich Nietzsche confirm the significance of rhetoric as technique is examined. After a synoptic survey of the contributions of Marx and Nietzsche, the emerging perspective offered in this chapter is contrasted with poststructuralism. Only then is it possible to present rhetoric as an agency of freedom, a technique through which persons express themselves, secure and defend rights, and challenge authority.

THE CLASSICAL DEBATE OVER RHETORIC

The mutually exclusive positions held by the sophists and Plato on every issue related to epistemology and rhetoric indicate the virulence of their opposition. Following Protagoras's doctrine of perception, sophism contends that all knowledge was relative to the individual.

Everyone knows things not as they are, but as they are in the moment of perception for him, and for him only: and they are in this moment with reference to him such as he represents them to himself. This is the meaning of the Protagorean relativism, according to which things are for every individual such as they appear to him.[3]

With this doctrine, Protagoras transfers the "problem of knowledge from the object to the subject," a move that calls into question the possibility of universal, transindividual truth.[4] If knowledge is valid then only for the one perceiving, as Protagoras posits, then the notion of universal validity must be forsaken. Eschewing absolute truth as unattainable, sophism prefers, instead, to define knowledge in terms of its practical implications.

Most important to sophism are the practical implications of knowledge for the conduct of political life. Anticipating the later Platonic notion of knowledge as an end in itself, sophism values knowledge only insofar as it allows persons to evaluate critically the conditions of life for the purpose of improving them. This commitment to pragmatic skepticism lies behind the sophistic critique of laws, customs, and institutions, all of which were formerly thought to rest on either natural imperatives or dicta from the gods. Whether their origin is seen to be in nature or divine decree, their most important quality is their immutability and intractability to reform.

The sophists counter this prevailing belief in immutable social forms by arguing that all laws, customs, and institutions are devised by humans, founded on conventions and, therefore, amenable to reform. Protagoras's injunction that the gods left all persons free and nature made no one a slave suggests sophism's commitment to self-determination and social reform, as does the fact that most sophistic discourse preaches "the value of the supreme Greek virtue, 'sophrosyne' (that we may translate as 'self control')."[5] To understand how this relativist epistemology joins with pragmatic skepticism to bring about social reform requires an explanation of the sophistic views of *logos* and rhetoric.

Sophism holds that no knowledge exists outside *logos*, understood as language and speech. If perception is the mechanism whereby humans apprehend sense data, language is the medium through which data are known and made communicable. Language does not, therefore, simply name or describe a phenomenon whose truth as been objectively demonstrated. On the contrary, language participates in and defines the phenomenon whose truth is at issue. Thus, sophism argues that things and persons appear as they are presented in language. Consequently, those who have command over language have command over the world of things and persons. What counts as truth, then, is what prevails when different perceptions of things and persons collide in argument. Stated differently, given conflicting accounts of an event, the account that is argued most effectively, and thereby adopted by the majority of listeners, will stand as truthful.

Having repudiated objective standards of truth, sophism turns to rhetoric as the means by which truth is established through the interrelated practices of refutation and legitimation. Sophism conceives rhetoric "primarily as a *techne* (art) whose medium is *logos* and whose double aim is *terpsis* (aesthetic pleasure) and *pistis* (belief)."[6] Borrowing from Martin Heidegger, whose work resonates with sophistic influences, language speaks the world and rhetoric funtions to elicit conviction. Note that it is through rhetoric that social laws may be challenged, for if order cannot be justified it may be refuted and replaced. Significantly, it is through rhetoric that the individual may exercise autonomy in the face of material advantage. Class, monetary privilege, and reputation matter less than the capacity to refute another's position and simultaneously present a compelling alternative.

In the end, sophism hinges on a conception of the subject as an autonomous individual who derives freedom from the potency of rhetoric. This sophistic understanding of rhetoric as a technique of liberation, critique, and change clashes with Plato's idealist stance toward language and knowledge.

Plato's opposition to sophism is thoroughgoing and no more evident than in his approach to epistemology and rhetoric. While conceding that Protagorean relativism does explain the sensible order of knowledge, Plato insists that everyday existence is secondary to questions of the "ideal," "being," and the "good." Attaining knowledge of being was both possible and necessary since only that knowledge has universal validity. Such knowledge is thought by Plato to transcend the sensible world and exist in the timeless realm of ideas where static perfection was the norm. Moreover, such knowledge is valued not for its practical import, but as an end in itself.[7]

Unlike the sophists, Plato is less concerned with individuals than with the perfection of the human species. Central to Plato's vision of perfection is the republic, the ideal social order where individual rights are subordinated to the state. As Eduard Zeller observes: "Of any personal rights or regard for the individual (except in so far as it is useful to the community) the *Republic* contains no mention."[8] Obviously, the sophists and Plato held divergent views on knowledge and the uses to which it may be put. Given these initial differences, it is not surprising that the sophists and Plato also disagree about the nature of language and rhetoric.

Plato does not grant *logos* the same importance as the sophists, and remains unconvinced about its constructive power. In contrast to sophism, Plato maintains that the inherent ambiguity of language impedes the search for absolutes. While language may yield probability statements about the sensible order, only the mind can penetrate the intelligible order to reveal the ideal form of a phenomenon. Truth is not based on consensus or beliefs engendered by rhetoric but instead on the "true reality of things."[9]

In light of Plato's attitude toward language, his view of rhetoric is not surprising. Plato defines rhetoric as a technique that centers on strategies like trickery and illusion.[10] Plato's dislike for rhetoric is displayed in his dialogues *Gorgias* and *Phaedrus*, where it indicts rhetoric for being sheerly a technique of persuasion. That Plato is a master rhetorician who employed all the sophistic devises of influence is first observed by Cicero. Cicero points out that Plato, through rhetorical skill and even distortion, convincingly counterposes his views against the sophists' for the sake of appearing to be the better thinker.

Hence, Plato uses the sophistic means of refutation and legitimation for the purpose of achieving superiority over his rivals. Like the sophists, Plato uses rhetoric to establish the truth of his case. Plato's duplicity is less important than what his dialogues reveal about the correctness of the sophistic position. That is, rhetoric cannot be avoided and must not be understood as simple ornamentation. Nonetheless, rhetoric is integral to language and the constitution of knowledge and truth. Plato may assert his freedom abstractly through the mind, but is is through rhetoric that his freedom is exercised. Similarly, it is through rhetoric that Plato's disagreements with the sophists are dramatized as well as his alternate position.

The foregoing contrast shows how differently rhetoric may be understood. Whereas the sophists define rhetoric in terms of its constitutive power to establish truth, Plato defines rhetoric as a deceptive artifice with no epistemic value. Over the centuries, however, it is Plato's definition that prevails. Indeed, his denunciations of the sophists saddles them with the wholly undeserved reputation as minor figures of no philosophic consequence. Beyond this unfortunate result, Plato's argument obscures the definitive role that rhetoric plays in philosophy. It remained for Marx and Nietzsche to discover anew both that rhetoric figures centrally in philosophy and that it can serve as a trenchant weapon of freedom.

RHETORIC AS IDEOLOGY AND POWER

Marx's understanding of rhetoric must be inferred, for he does not address the subject directly. Nevertheless, his discussion of ideology, especially in *The German Ideology*, illustrates that rhetoric may either serve or challenge the established order. To explain, ideology is a form of rhetorical *praxis* that may either protect or transform the social relations of production. When serving the established order, ideology makes existing power arrangements appear "natural" and convincing. Ideology of this sort is said to "form the ultimate explanatory rhetoric of a society."[11] To be effective, such explanatory rhetoric must be well constructed, seem logical and coherent, and be able to adapt to changing circumstances. Additionally, such ideology must be efficiently disseminated and cogently advocated so that it never appears problematic.[12] In short, this kind of ideology fits well with part of the sophistic position, for it works to define reality and legitimize a particular rendition of order.

The second kind of ideology, which Marx terms "revolutionary," also fits well with the sophistic position. Revolutionary ideology questions critically the established order, particularly all attempts to naturalize inequities and class divisions. This is similar to the sophist's attack on the supposedly natural or divine foundations for Greek laws and institutions. In brief, revolutionary ideology demands justification for the hegemony of the established order and ultimately calls for its overthrow. Calling for a new order requires the use of rhetoric to advance a convincing picture of an alternate social reality. By this process of critique, revolutionary ideology unmasks the false ideology of the established order and replaces it with a more defensible ideological formation. Ideology, therefore, cannot be eradicated, for in Louis Althusser's account, "it is a structure essential to the historical life of societies."[13] Precisely this view underlies Althusser's claim that "only the existence and recognition of its [ideology's] necessity enable us to act on ideology and transform ideology into an instrument of deliberate action on history."[14]

While Marx speaks of rhetoric only implicitly, obviously ideology represents a rhetorical technique. Significantly, revolutionary ideology functions as rhetoric to inspire critique and change, thereby permitting individuals to act freely on history. Although Marx begins to disentangle the relationships between ideology and rhetoric, this task is brought to completion by Nietzsche.

Nietzsche views rhetoric in a manner similar to the sophists. For instance, he scorns as "perverse and nonsensical" the Platonic quest for a world of true being which transcends change, and prefers, instead, the sophistic view that only the world of "conditional relations" can be known.[15] With Protagoras, Nietzsche concurs that knowledge is always "perspectival." Hence Richard Schacht's observation that Nietzsche "not only repudiates the very idea of 'absolute knowledge' and of 'truth' as an exact correspondence to reality, but also maintains that 'truth' is inescapably perspectival, and 'knowledge' essentially interpretive."[16] Thus, knowing cannot be disinterested nor knowledge universal because the world is related inextricably to human values. Nietzsche's stand on knowledge leads him to conclude that one cannot establish facts in themselves, but only facts "in the context of interpretation."[17] Furthermore, "contexts of interpretation" are never fixed, and as such the "facts" of which they are constitutive are similarly impermanent. Like the sophists, Nietzsche prizes interpretive knowledge that "relates to the attainment of practical objectives in our dealings with the world and others."[18] Knowledge for Neitzsche is not found in a rarefied pursuit of being but represents a "tool of power" that enables persons to question freely accepted norms.

Further binding Nietzsche to the sophists is their shared conception of the tales that language and rhetoric play in the promulgation of knowledge. Knowledge and language are linked inextricably to the extent that linguistic practices establish the conditions under which truth is formulated. Linguistic practices outline the conventions and criteria by which concepts and propositions are judged. This means that persons do not discover the truth and then resort to language to communicate it. Rather, truth is created through the advancement and legitimation of interpretations. Consider Nietzsche's account:

"Truth" is therefore not something there, that might be found or discovered—but something that must be created and that gives a name to a process, or rather to a will to overcome that has in itself no end—introducing truth, as a "processus in infinitum," an active determining—not a becoming—conscious of something that is in itself firm and determined.[19]

Nietzsche urges philosophers no longer to "accept concepts as a gift . . . but first make and create them, present them and make them convincing."[20] Thus, Nietzsche agrees with the sophists that truth is negotiated, not proven, and founded on those interpretations judged most "convincing."

At the core of Nietzsche's approach to truth is the sophistic idea that truth is constituted through the use of language.

What therefore is truth? A flexible army of metaphors, metonymies, anthropomorphisms, in short, a sum of human relations, which have been poetically and rhetorically intensified, transformed, bejeweled, and which after long usage seem to a people to be fixed, canonical, and binding.[21]

Rhetoric is intimately united with the practices by which truth is created, presented, and negotiated in a context of differing interpretations. It is rhetorical efficacy that allows an interpretation to withstand negotiation and refutation and finally to emerge as dominant. Nietzsche's concept of the "will to power" explains an individual's drive to declare, through the agencies of rhetoric, his or her interpretation as dominant. Dominance resides not in truth but in the rhetorical power to reinforce a particular interpretation.

Animating his concept of the will to power is Nietzsche's metaphor of the "mutual struggle," whereby varying interpretations are "locked in combat with each other" for supremacy.[22] And freedom for Nietzsche consists of "assuming responsibility" for one's viewpoint in this struggle, and having the persistence to maintain this perspective in the face of "resistance." Uncritical believers are derogated by Nietzsche who claims that they lack the will to think as "free spirits."[23] Nietzsche's approach to freedom resembles that of sophists because its focus is the individual. Karl Jaspers captures well the "challenge" attendant to living this Nietzschean freedom: "Its challenge is tremendous, for the entire burden is laid upon the individual. He requires each of us to follow the insecure and thus dangerous new path of the individual. . . . "[24]

Taken together, Marx and Nietzsche can be seen as the inheritors of the legacy of sophism. Nietzsche, Marx, and the sophists stress the pivotal nature of rhetoric as technique. In the work of these writers, rhetoric represents much more than figural embellishment for it serves an epistemic function that makes possible the exercise of freedom, critique, and change. Nonetheless, recently this viewpoint has been distorted by those who equate rhetorical technique with technology, thereby stripping language of its power to shape the world.

RHETORIC AS TECHNIQUE, AS AGAINST RHETORIC AS TECHNOCRACY

Ellul defines technocracy as a "regime," in which "power is exercised by technicians."[25] Currently, poststructuralism qualifies as such a "regime," inasmuch as its adherents are self-described technicians who wield power through their deconstructive method. Thematically, poststructuralism seems to overlap with the perspective offered by the sophists, Marx, and Nietzsche, for poststructuralism originates with skepticism and emphasizes that interpretation should be "liberated, creative, producing the meanings that it makes rather than discovers."[26] Additionally, poststructuralism celebrates the plurality of meaning and understands language to constitute knowledge. Likewise, language is conceived as "always, at once, and originarily, figural or rhetorical, rather than referential or representational."[27]

Practically, however, distinctions between poststructuralists and writers such as Nietzsche, Marx, and the sophists begin to surface. Contrary to the work of these authors, poststructuralism results in a type of anarchy that is anathema to reform. Although truth is perspectival and momentary, some style of knowledge is necessary for change.

Even Nietzsche argues that some criteria, variable and inexact as they may be, are essential if change is to be wrought. For instance, one criterion that Nietzsche recommends, which is clearly within the purview of rhetoric as technique, is the "aptness of metaphor."

The aptness of a metaphor in ordinary discourse obviously depends in no small measure upon its resonance for a group of users of a language.... Its ability to articulate and convey something about that which is spoken of is a function of the exploitability of associations they are capable of appreciating; and this presupposes the existence of a discursive context or perspective.[28]

Nietzsche rehabilitates knowledge and portrays it as conditioned by the "discursive context" of language. That is, within the context of knowing are multiple viewpoints and the more completely these perspectives are entertained—"the forms of interaction into which the thing is capable of entering"—the more that is disclosed about both the act of knowing and the objects of knowledge.[29] Nietzsche is not implying that knowledge can be achieved outside of a perspective, but only that knowers should remain self-conscious in the act of knowing. Yet no matter how rigorously self-conscious a person may be, the knowledge generated remains conditioned by its human origins. In this way, Nietzsche "resurrects the notion of the possibility of knowledge in modified form, as the conditioned apprehension of the conditioned."[30] Assuming that such conditional knowledge can be gained, the knower must still, through rhetoric, "compel the . . . other drives to accept as a norm" this viewpoint.[31]

In addition, poststructuralism describes the knowing subject as positioned and determined by codes that cannot be controlled. While the person described by the sophists, Marx, and Nietzsche cannot escape the net of language and its defining tropes, persons operate with some degree of autonomy within these bounds. The fact that poststructuralists have identified the putative effects of language suggests that the subject's latitude of autonomy is wider than their arguments indicate. Nonetheless, further differences arise with poststructuralism. Poststructuralists use rhetorical analysis for the deconstructive end of rewriting and reestablishing control over the text. By confining their attention only to texts, following Jacques Derrida's slogan "there is nothing outside the text," poststructuralists spin out reading after reading with little purpose beyond exhibiting a technocratic mastery of paradox and style.[32] Hence, critique in the poststructuralist sense is done in "historical isolation, as though the text were a closed system."[33] Political and ethical questions such as those raised by the sophists, Marx, and Nietzsche do not concern the poststructuralists. Rhetoric as technique in the poststructuralist sense, then, is a sterile exercise in the technological manipulation of meaning. Texts are merely manipulated in order to rearrange their structure, while the world and its meaning are obscured. In the final analysis, poststructuralism is a technocracy with no point of reference beyond the intricacies of the text.

Conversely, the perspective offered by the sophists, Marx, and Nietzsche appreciates critique because of the constructive consequences it may produce. While poststructuralism remains conveniently "text bound," these writers treat rhetoric as a technique for confronting questions beyond the text. Accordingly, their view of rhetoric urges social engagement, however distanced a text may appear to be from the world of persons. Finally, they employ rhetoric as a technique to engender skepticism and freedom, thereby promoting critique and worthy reform. Simply put, the sophists, Marx, and Nietzsche view rhetoric as a technique of social engagement as opposed to a technology of control.

NOTES

1. Paul de Man, *Allegories of Reading: Figural Language in Rousseau, Nietzsche, Rilke, and Proust* (New Haven, Conn.: Yale University Press, 1979), p. 300.

2. Hayden White, *Tropics of Discourse: Essays in Cultural Criticism* (Baltimore: John Hopkins University Press, 1978).

3. Wilhelm Windelband, *A History of Philosophy*, trans. James H. Tufts (New York: Harper and Brothers, 1958), p. 92.

4. Eduard Zeller, *Outlines of the History of Greek Philosophy*, trans. L. R. Palmer (New York: Meridian Books , 1964), p. 98.

5. Bromley Smith, "Corax and Probability," in Lionel Crocker and Paul A. Carmack, eds., *Readings in Rhetoric* (Springfield, Ill.: Charles C. Thomas, 1965), p. 45.

6. John Poulakos, "Toward a Sophistic Definition of Rhetoric," *Philosophy and Rhetoric* 16 (Winter 1983): 36.

7. This interpretation of Plato derives from Benjamin Jowett's translation of the *Republic*. *Plato's Republic* (New York: Airmont Publishing Company, 1968).

8. Zeller, *Outlines of the History of Greek Philosophy*, p. 160.

9. *Plato's Republic*, p. 299.

10. Throughout the *Gorgias*, Plato propounds this argument regarding the baseness of rhetoric. See Plato, *Gorgias*, trans. Walter Hamilton (New York: Penguin Books, 1979).

11. Morse Peckham, *Explanation and Power* (New York: Seabury Press, 1979), p. 222.

12. Rosalind Coward and John Ellis, *Language and Materialism* (Boston: Routledge & Kegan Paul, 1977), pp. 78–79.

13. Louis Althusser, *For Marx*, trans. Ben Brewster (New York: Vintage Books, 1970), p. 232.

14. Ibid.

15. Friedrich W. Nietzsche, *The Will to Power*, trans. Walter Kaufmann (New York: Vintage Books, 1968), p. 556.

16. Richard Schacht, *Nietzsche* (Boston: Routledge & Kegan Paul, 1983), p. 95.

17. Nietzsche, *Will to Power*, p. 481.

18. Schacht, *Nietzsche*, p. 87.

19. Nietzsche, *Will to Power*, p. 552.

20. Ibid., p. 412.

21. Friedrich W. Nietzsche, "On Truth and Lie in an Extra-moral Sense," in Walter Kaufmann, ed., *The Portable Nietzsche* (New York: Penguin Books, 1976), pp. 46–47.

22. Arthur Danto, "Nietzsche's Perspectivism," in Robert C. Solomon, ed., *Nietzsche* (New York: Anchor Books, 1973), p. 40.

23. Friedrich W. Nietzsche, *Beyond Good and Evil*, trans. by Walter Kaufmann (New York: Vintage Books, 1966), p. 29.

24. Karl Jaspers, *Nietzsche: An Introduction to the Understanding of His Philosophical Activity* (Tucson: University of Arizona Press, 1965), p. 158.

25. Jacques Ellul, "Technique, Institutions, and Awareness," *The American Behavioral Scientist* 6 (July/August 1968): 39.

26. M. H. Abrams, "How to Do Things with Texts," *Partisan Review* 44, no. 4 (1979): 568.

27. Vincent B. Leitch, *Deconstructive Criticism* (New York: Columbia University Press, 1983), p. 47.

28. Schacht, *Nietzsche*, p. 100.

29. Ibid., p. 101.

30. Ibid., p. 102.

31. Nietzsche, *The Will to Power*, p. 481.

32. Richard Rorty, "Derrida on Language, Being and Abnormal Philosophy," *Journal of Philosophy* 74, no. 11 (November 1977): 675.

33. Walter J. Ong, *Orality and Literacy* (New York: Methuen, 1982), p. 169.

13

Overcoming Communicative Incompetence in the Global Communication Order: The Case of Technology Transfer

Joseph J. Pilotta and Tim L. Widman

The price of social structural and technological development is tele-communication. Telecommunication exercises a powerful impact on all societal sub-systems by affecting the ways they fulfill their traditional functions, particularly the way change is understood. This power to alter human temporality has been described by Emilio Filippi as a central feature of technology "transfer" in developing countries. As he writes:

The telecommunication and computer revolutions on the one hand bring people close together and on the other isolate them. They bring them closer because simultaneously the world over we are aware of what is happening elsewhere. But at the same time the manipulation of these mechanisms—the "mission control," if you will—that manages all of this isolates human beings. It converts them into objects of communication, not subjects of communication. This is a dramatic dehumanization.[1]

As soon as information is disclosed, a type of telecommunication public is created, as a common knowledge base is necessary for messages to be comprehended.[2] Thus, the global simultaneity accompanying telecommunication accelerates expectations that may or may not be compatible with the performances of local social functions vital to developing countries. In other words, the social premise of what others are supposed to know changes the dimensions of experience and action.[3] Because all persons are supposed to be a part of the telecommunication order, they are assumed to share a common knowledge base.

The global communication industry presents a Janus face. Although telecommunication establishes a global society, at the same time separate spheres of activity are created and reinforced. The results are twofold: any individualized interpretation of the meaning of communication is absent, as any one version becomes but a component in a global mystery play, while the interdependence of interpretations is increased.

This is not the philosophers' trap of the contradiction between the universal and the particular, but rather the process whereby the particular is deprecated because it is not universal. Thus, telecommunication may be viewed as creating alienation in the form of communicative incompetence, as persons are treated as objects rather than subjects. Alienation is a process whereby activity is channeled into nominally independent spheres, with each of these domains subordinated to a scheme dictated by the telecommunication order. The chief effect of this on developing countries is a contraction of their experiential horizons that seriously limits the range of available social, cultural, economic, and political possibilities, thus thwarting future development. A particular society, in this sense, is subordinated to the norms operating to organize the global order.

The issue of "underdeveloped countries" has become volatile within the framework of a global communication system.[4] A "free flow" information policy has pitted the universal against the particular on a global scale, thus robbing the particular of its identity.[5] This policy has been summarized trenchantly by Kwame Nkrumah: "Europeans insist upon the denial that we are an historic people."[6] Accordingly, communicative incompetence is a process within the structure of a global communication system, whereby the particular is transformed into the universal. Simply put, the modern global communication industry has as its defining characteristic the socialization or universalization of the world. Each society is effectively particular, yet only within the technologically socialized totality. Furthermore, each attempts to realize the universal in its activity by generalizing what it does to the social totality.

Thus, communication technology does not represent a limited form of consciousness within a given social formation but is the very structure of global functional differentiation. The demand for totality built into its structure becomes the demand for a universal truth. Yet the resulting alienation cannot be overcome without a redefinition of the task of theory, specifically communication theory. This chapter outlines a view of communication that does not totalize and reify the norms of communication (that is, the universal), thus enabling information to be transferred throughout the world in a nonrepressive manner.[7] This theoretical model combines a polycentrist dialogical view of human communication, as advanced by Bernhard Waldenfels,[8] with a critical sociological and phenomenological perspective, based on the work of Alfred Schutz[9] and Jurgen Habermas,[10] and a structural-integrative position on social change.[11]

INTERCULTURAL COMMUNICATION AND TECHNOLOGY TRANSFER

From the standpoint of intercultural communication, an important problem relates to the way in which technology is understood and subsequently transmitted to recipient cultures. The central difficulty is that technology's current mode of rational-scientific legitimation encourages a style of intercultural delivery and implementation that is insensitive to cultural exigencies and, thus, subverts existing social meanings and practices. In its present form, the intercultural transfer of technology presupposes a model of communication that is linear and asymmetrical. As Figure 1 illustrates, this source of bias operates at both the level of technical knowledge and cultural meanings. The implications of this become clear when it is illustrated how technology is interpreted and introduced across cultures.

Because of its scientific status, technology is thought to be abstract and thus essentially independent of the contingencies associated with human social interaction. Because technology is rooted in scientific detachment, the values implicit in it are assumed to have universal validity. Hence, technology is endowed with an "objective" appearance, which encourages the belief that it represents pure or rational knowledge. In short, technology appears to have a destiny of its own. Additionally, its *a priori*, rationalist presuppositions encourage donor nations to believe that so-called developing ones can be drawn unproblematically into the global history outlined by a technical culture. This conviction elevates the technological competence possessed by donor nations to an abstract standard, against which cultural self-worth is assessed. The view of technological competence held by donor nations leads them to

Figure 1
Intercultural Transfer of Technology

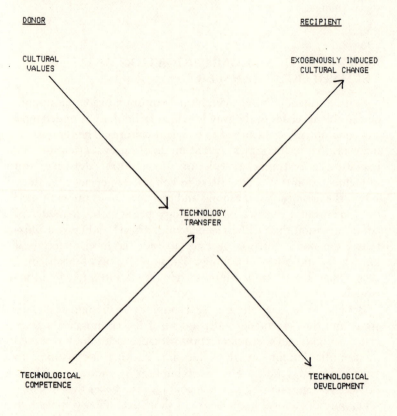

DONOR

RECIPIENT

CULTURAL
VALUES

EXOGENOUSLY INDUCED
CULTURAL CHANGE

TECHNOLOGY
TRANSFER

TECHNOLOGICAL
COMPETENCE

TECHNOLOGICAL
DEVELOPMENT

practice a tutelary commercialism with respect to the diffusion of their technologies around the world.

This commodifying of technological competence distorts the historical experience and self-regard of recipient groups by shaping their cognitive categories according to the demands of technological reason. Because the political economy of the information age is fueled by knowledge and ideas, the production and use of technology presupposes that recipient societies have been socialized appropriately to understand technological values and imperatives. The following statement describes this problem:

But there can be no doubt that in the North-South arena, the North has far, far more than its share of the "good lawyers." Academia, the media, and government spokesmen have together so swamped the advocates for the South with their "too crude" arguments that they have created a mood within which Southern arguments are almost automatically ascribed to "unreason," or "bad economics"; they are assumed to be illegitimate almost as soon as they are made, and it becomes Northern sport to see who can first firmly prove them so. The transnationalism of knowledge through post-graduate training, scholarly journals, and the press furthers the legitimization of Northern positions, and extends even into the academic institutions and governmental offices of the South. Intellectual hegemony may be no less powerful and enduring than any other kind.[12]

Market domination of intellectual raw materials completes the cycle necessary for information commodity exchange. Although donor countries tend to monopolize technical knowledge, a small group of trained persons in recipient countries is essential for providing the linkages necessary for technological transfer. Yet the ever present indebtedness, if not unfailing allegiance, of the overseas educated elite to their mentors—educationally, technically, and fiscally—ensures a stable free-flow framework for the information economy. The result of this is cultural domination by a select few who possess the information required to operate a technological society.

Technological mastery tacitly assumes cultural chauvinism, however benevolent. Cultural intervention, through knowledge transfer, includes not simply the diffusion of technical material and trained scientists, it also involves the diffusion of culturally specific meanings and historically acquired structural interpretations of reality that underpin technology. To export technology is to export meaning: To export meaning is to export culture and history. According to Johan Galtung:

There is more to techniques than meets the naked eye. There is a whole social structure operating internationally, locally, and one of a very specific kind, together with a cognitive structure of deep-lying assumptions about the organization of space and time and knowledge, of human relations and relations with nature, that combine with the techniques to constitute technology. Without at least a substantial portion of these structures, the technique cannot operate. Moreover, the social structure is one that places . . . the metropoles of the West in the center, and the cognitive structure confers legitimacy on this: it decrees that those who are farthest advanced in knowledge, skills and hardware ought, and indeed deserve to be, in the center, or at the top of the pyramid. The techniques reinforce that pyramid, and the pyramid, the social structure, serves to generate new techniques that do not upset the structure.[13]

Obviously, as long as the standards of development are set unilaterally by the "developed" nations, conflict will persist between the countries that "have arrived" and those that are perpetually "on the way."

CULTURAL RELEVANCE AND COMMUNICATIVE COMPETENCE

In recent years, scholars working in the area of development have become sensitive to the use of Western theoretical paradigms in intercultural studies. Many concur with one of the leading scholars in the field of development, Everette Rogers, who observes that "as definitions of development, and actual development programs, stress equality of distribution, popular participation in decentralized activities, self-development, etc., the concepts and methods of diffusion inquiry must change appropriately."[14]

Rogers summarizes the newer conception of development as:

a widely participatory process of social change in a society intended to bring about both social and material advancement (including greater equality, freedom, and other valued qualities) for the majority of the people through their gaining greater control over their environment.[15]

As should be noted, Rogers refers to participation, equality, and freedom as central to proper development.

If development programs ought to promote these qualities, then the question becomes how can technical assistance projects contribute to their realization? Yet these qualities are not simply the goals of diffusion as if they represented a variety of desirable social outcomes. Instead, they must be integrated into the communication process, whereby knowledge is exchanged. Freedom, equality, and participation are social-structural, relational, and communicational dimensions that demand reciprocity and mutual understanding among individual social actors. Most important is that a model for the intercultural communication of technology-based polycentricity and dialogue offers an alternative to one grounded in communicative asymmetry. As Galtung notes:

Given the propensity of the system, the present author is led to the conclusion that it is much easier and more productive to push forward toward a meaningful global interdependence on the communication side than on the economic side. With the former, it is not too impossible to proceed from manipulation via a winner/loser debate to a dialogue. With the latter, it seems almost impossible to arrive at an exchange relation that is not exploitive one way or the other.[16]

As Figure 2 illustrates, this dialogical approach is more complicated, but more rich than the linear orientation. Yet dialogue between countries is essential for the nonrepressive transfer of technology. Thus, the remainder of this chapter is devoted to discussing this dialogical model.

Technological assistance influences a society's symbolic expressions. Specifically, technology carries its own cultural system of relevances through which people view themselves and interpret others. The delivery of technological implements and knowledge across cultural boundaries is, therefore, an intermixing of cultures and schemes of relevance. Simply put, the recipient of technology encounters "foreign" semiotic conventions. Effective and culturally responsible technological aid, therefore, requires an assessment of the recipient culture's criteria of relevance. In turn, determining the relevance of technical information calls for an intercultural dialogue that addresses the value and symbolic components of *all* participants

Figure 2
Dialogical Approach to Technology Transfer

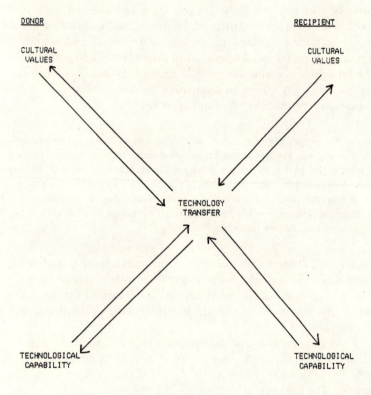

in the information exchange. This dialogue allows technical input to be adjusted to cultural norms.

Since every human being lives in a cultural system of relevances, knowledge about a society's values is integral for planning a technology transfer strategy. Before human science can act responsibly in the world community, the cultural presuppositions that influence the process of technological transfer must be identified. Interculturally competent communication of technology requires that the system of relevance assumed by technology must be clarified; the system of relevance operative within the recipient population must be assessed; and these systems must be aligned. These conditions must be satisfied if technology transfer is to respect the cultural integrity of developing nations.[17] Clearly, the objective of communicatively competent technology transfer is to avoid the one-sided imposition of foreign values upon the recipient culture. Yet only when technologies are understood as vehicles of meaning can the vicious cycle of cultural domination and lopsided development be broken, which is endemic to many of the current technical assistance programs.

The concept of "relevance" designates a composite of values, their interconnectedness, and the functions they have in a society. Relevance is "what matters" to a specific socio–cultural group, including the history of that group's past commitments and future possibilities.[18] Relevance functions to determine which facts, events, or problems are treated as valuable and to provide a scheme of interpretation that specifies the parameters of meaningful behavior and discourse. Donor nations can be responsive and responsible to another culture only if they adequately understand their own system of relevances and, accordingly, recognize how it affects another culture. The possibility for successful international communication transactions rests upon establishing congruence between interculturally pertinent relevances. This means that a common scheme of interpretation and orientation must be found, one shared by the deliverer of a technology and its receiver. In fact, intercultural relevance is the key criterion for enhancing technology transfer in the international community.

It must be remembered that technology does not have to be an irresistible force that undermines a culture's identity; however, its present abstract and reified power can seriously undermine a recipient society. Therefore, a rational and responsible attitude toward the "problem" of technology transfer requires that the system of relevancies presupposed by technology be examined in light of the existing cultural standards of the recipient. In other words, technology must be implemented within the social and cultural "space" offered by a recipient society. Accomplishing this difficult task requires a polycentric viewpoint that is sensitive to the meaning of technology within the relevance framework of a recipient culture.

THE POLYCENTRIC FRAMEWORK OF
CULTURAL DIALOGUE

The polycentric standpoint embraces two important principles. First, it calls attention to the qualitative historical *uniqueness* of human cultural experiences. As the result, the analysis of cultural differences is elevated to a central role in all phases of intercultural knowledge exchange. Second, the polycentric standpoint gives legitimacy to the role cognition plays in shaping the social world. This means that detached universalistic objectivism, a uniquely Western cognitive style, has validity only within a limited epistemological perspective of world interpretation. By granting validity to the truth claims advanced by various cognitive styles, the resulting systems of meaning can become thematic and assessed in their own terms. Meanings, in this sense, are relative.

In place of tacit assumptions held about the universal nature of the human essence and transcultural truth, the principle of "quintessential cultural differentness" becomes the first order axiom of cultural exchange. In other words, the principle for cross–cultural comparisons is the recognition of difference. This is in contrast to the Western tradition that predicates all comparisons on similarity as opposed to "differentness."[19] This means that a common understanding can be reached through an appreciation of differences as opposed to being based on a set of norms that are assumed to be universal. Consequently, "what" and "how" something becomes meaningful is understood to result from cultural self-selection.[20] The complicated interdependence of the many elements of a communication system has been confirmed by the complex way knowledge exchange changes societies, for almost every attempt to use technological correctives results in indirect repercussions for the recipient society.

Even though the complexity and unpredictability of cultural communication systems create difficulties for technological intervention, these very same properties provide the keys to preserving the cultural integrity of societies. Because a culture's memory contains more than can be experienced or expressed at any moment, common threads of meaning are visible despite periods of pronounced controversy and cultural transformation.[21] For as evolutionary forces drive the cultural communication system toward an increasingly differentiated sign system, the multivalent character of a culture's relevancies is exposed. In this sense, social differentiation reveals a culture to be an organization of differences. At the boundary of these differences is where mutual recognition occurs. Hence, difference can serve as the basis of communication and technology transfer. Once the monolithic image of culture is shattered, the recognition of difference becomes imperative for successful communication.

Acknowledgment of cultural uniqueness carries with it a serious concern for cultural autonomy. Where the polycentrist attitude toward knowledge exchange is operative, a foreign culture's meanings are no longer regarded as an irrelevant subjective datum. Instead, a structural obligation comes into play that promotes intercultural dialogue: The two partners become communicatively accountable to one another by acknowledging the coequal value of all symbols.[22] Thus, the recognition of difference fosters mutual understanding.

One important implication of this redefinition of the communication relationship involves a reevaluation of the role that needs play in developmental assistance projects. Typically, needs are taken to represent objective insufficiencies that can be identified empirically. Thus, needs-assessment techniques are technologies that operate most often on the basis of preestablished Western assumptions about social and cultural well-being. In turn, remedial technology is prescribed in terms of these abstract empirical needs.

By contrast, according to the polycentric viewpoint, "needs" are symbolic and specified according to the relevance structures rooted in the cognitive activities that link a culture's future with its past. Therefore, needs delineate culturally specific boundary-maintenance functions, which enable a society to determine what is socially possible and necessary. When assessing needs polycentrically, these boundary-maintenance functions are identified as the point of reference for establishing the types of technology that are most appropriate. Therefore, recipient self-determination and self-selection must be encouraged for the purpose of identifying needs reliably in addition to discriminating accurately the proper remedies for these deficiencies.

Given the requirements of dialogue, a recipient society's cultural assumptions specify what is meant by a need. Thus, according to an interculturally established definition of need, a recipient culture is best able to select the most appropriate technological correctives. And as a result of revealing the culturally specific form of a need, full participation of a recipient society in defining the scope of appropriate technology is encouraged, for this presupposes that all participants possess the credentials required to negotiate the particulars of a transfer agreement in terms of their respective frames of relevance. This dialogue contains three structural components: the competencies of the participants, common points of reference, and a framework for negotiation.

A polycentric foundation of dialogue gives rise to a consideration that is crucial for the intercultural communication of technology: The meaning of social change may be perceived quite differently by different cultures. Typically, the donor will take for granted the meanings embodied in technology and direct attention to the cultural modifications required for a technique to be successfully implemented in another country. In other words, the donor will regard disruption as the effect of technology and anticipate some measure of change in the values, economic institutions, or social organization of the recipient. The recipient culture, on the other hand, will regard technology as disruptive but treat it as a cause of disorder. Accordingly, presupposed cultural values must be made relative and brought into play, so that a shared understanding about the problem of technology can be reached. As the participants share information and priorities with one another, a sense of mutuality can be achieved about how technology should be instituted.

INTERCULTURAL COMMUNICATIVE ACCOUNTABILITY

The existing alternative to making problems relative is to continue to conceal the dimensions of time and tradition operating in culture. To persist in this manner perpetuates donor paternalism by withholding from recipient cultures the information they need to activate their own capabilities. Such communication practices perpetuate the attitude expressed earlier by Filippi, when he stated that developing nations are treated as objects rather than subjects of communication. What can be done?

A research procedure premised on communicative accountability illuminates, from both the empirical and discursive points of view, the dynamic properties of a social situation and engages the citizenry in an open-ended dialogue about the accuracy, appropriateness, and value of a particular developmental policy. This procedure makes three assumptions: It is necessary that research and its outcomes establish social knowledge that reflects community interests; research involving technical assistance, or policy, must be responsive to the perceived needs and concerns of the researched population; and research must not obstruct, or attenuate, but promote self-determination. In short, researchers must acknowledge their participation within the meaning configurations of a social-cultural life world and actively invoke this experiential *a priori* as the criterion for assessing the validity of research.

An immediate consequence of this viewpoint is the elevation of social interpretation to a prominent position from the standpoint of both researchers and the population that is studied. This methodological premise is operationalized as *enablement*. It is against the background of enablement that social life "emerges as a product-producer, the locus where necessity can turn into concrete liberty."[23] This concrete actualization of the research process generates a historical and ethical partnership out of the researcher/subject association as a cooperative "working-out" of a future. A cultural world is never again seen as an object of experience, rather, it is viewed as constituted through human action. This new communicative liaison of researcher/subject is founded upon a mutual orientation toward solving a problem within the system of cultural relevancies operative in a particular society. Thus, the citizenry is encouraged to solve its own problems, which is at the heart of enablement.

A second consequence of communicative accountability is the employment of social relevance as the standard for guiding the selection of intervention strategies. This means that a recipient community knows best its own situation, thus requiring that all research be ratified by the citizenry. At the same time, research strategies must mobilize the recipient's self-understanding, for uncritical empathy can result in domination. As Alphonso Lingis observes:

It if is only our needs and wants that get articulated in signs, in hard signals, that is not only because it is the only common form of our impulses that can be understood by others, but because the others want to hear only our needs and lacks. For our needs are apprehended by others as appeals to themselves, expressions of dependence upon them, declarations of subservience, invitations to subjugation. It is through our needs and lacks that we appeal to the will in the others—the will to power in the others, the will to dominate.[24]

Such domination within technology transfer and knowledge exchange is only too well known in the form of dependency theory. Accordingly, when dealing with social and individual needs it is often assumed that a corrective cannot be forthcoming from the existing cultural conditions because it is precisely these that are deemed inadequate. Such a judgment is grounded on the belief that persons cannot redirect themselves and thus must turn over their future to experts. Contrary to this, research that promotes recipient autonomy provides an avenue for preventing interpersonal participation from becoming subtly transmuted into interpersonal domination.

As operationalized within the research process, communicative accountability assumes the form of communicatively constituted intersubjectivity. It is not the persons, the private intentions of communicators, or the objective social circumstance, but instead shared social meanings that are the focus of dialogical research.[25]

CONCLUSION

An intercultural, dialogical approach to communication makes possible cooperative and effective technology transfer, as a result of taking seriously social engagement for the purpose of promoting cultural self-determination among developing nations. Within this context it is necessary to pose questions such as: Why technology? Why technology transfer? Who determines the form and content of technology transfer? What role should indigenous technology play in social development?

But questions such as these can only be asked when a polycentric basis of cultural negotiation is kept squarely at the center of the exchange process. However, the essence of science consists in the formulation of these types of informed critical questions. The social reality of science, additionally, stipulates that intellectual progress cannot be made without peer recognition of the legitimacy of scientific questions. Yet as long as the developed nations maintain their guardianship over the domain of legitimate argumentation, Western interests will dictate the aims of scientific reason, for the pluralization of the world requires that intellectual autonomy be fostered. Of course, the West's benevolent imperialism prolongs its domination of developing nations, by reserving for them a secure place at the periphery of the technological revolution. Mostly, it promotes an insidious strain of cultural chauvinism because the West alone has the knowledge to plan technology and make it work. In short, the developed nations have been conquered by the domain of acceptable technological *praxis*.

NOTES

1. Emilio Filippi, "Very Serious Concerns...," *World Press Review* (December 1983): 39.

2. Johan Galtung, "Images of the World in the Year 2000: A Synthesis of the Marginals of the Ten Nations Study," paper presented at the Seventh World Congress of Sociology (Varna, 1983).

3. Niklas Luhmann, "The Future Cannot Begin," in Luhmann, *The Differentiation of Society*, trans. Stephen Holmes and Charles Larmore (New York: Columbia University Press, 1982), pp. 271–288.

4. Niklas Luhmann, "World-Time and System History," *Differentiation*, pp. 289–323.

5. Herbert I. Schiller, *Who Knows: Information in the Age of Fortune 500* (Norwood, N.J.: Ablex, 1981).

6. Kwame Nkrumah, *Revolutionary Path* (London: Panaf Books, 1973), p. 207.

7. Joseph Pilotta and Tim Widman, "Intercultural Relevance and Technology Transfer: A Communicative Competence Approach," paper presented at International Communication Association, Dallas, May 1983.

8. Bernhard Waldenfels, *Das Zwischenreich des Dialogs* (Den Haag: Nijhoff, 1971); *Der Spielraum des Verhaltens* (Frankfurt: Suhrkamp, 1980).

9. Alfred Schutz, "Equality and the Meaning Structure of the Social World," in E. A. Bronderson, ed., *Collected Papers II: Studies in Social*

Theory (The Hague: Martinus Hijhoff, 1964, pp. 226–276, *The Phenomenology of the Social World*, trans. G. Walsh and F. Lehnert (Evanston, Ill.: Northwestern University Press, 1967).

10. Jurgen Habermas, *Knowledge and Human Interests*, trans. Jeremy Shapiro (Boston: Beacon Press, 1971), *Legitimation Crisis*, trans. Thomas McCarthy (Boston: Beacon Press, 1975), *Communication and the Evolution of Society*, trans. Thomas McCarthy (Boston: Beacon Press, 1979).

11. Niklas Luhmann, *Soziologische Aufklarung: Aufsatze zur Theorie sozialer Systeme* (Kohn: Westdeutscher Verlag, 1970). Jean Gebser, *Everpresent Origin*, trans. A. Mickunas and N. Barstad (Athens: Ohio University Press, 1984).

12. "Recommendations for Further Research and Activity," *International Development Research* 1 (Spring 1980): 39.

13. Johan Galtung, *Development, Environment and Technology: Towards a Technology for Self-Reliance*, United Nations Conference on Trade and Development (New York: United Nations, 1979), p. 1.

14. Everette Rogers, "Innovation in Organizations: New Research Approaches," paper presented at American Political Science Association, San Francisco, September 1975, p. 31.

15. Everette Rogers, "The Rise and Fall of the Dominant Paradigm," *Journal of Communication* (Winter 1978): 68. See as well Everette Rogers and D. Lawrence Kincaid, *Communication Networks: Toward a New Research Paradigm* (New York: Free Press, 1983).

16. Johan Galtung, "The New International Order: Economics and Communication," in M. Jussamalta and D. M. Laberton, eds., *Communication Economics and Development* (Elmsford, N.Y.: Pergamon Press, 1982), p. 142.

17. Compare Cees Hamelink, *Cultural Autonomy in Global Communication* (New York: Longman, 1983).

18. Maurice Natanson, *The Journeying Self: A Study in Philosophy and Social Role* (Reading, Penn.: Addison-Wesley, 1970), p. 99.

19. Western metaphysics has long conceptualized "differentness" as dissimilarity; the proposed intercultural logic conceives similarity as "non-differentness." The traditional Western orientation toward unity and sameness becomes exacerbated in the cultural sphere because the Western culture typically forms the unspoken *tertium compartionis*.

20. Niklas Luhmann, *Macht* (Stuttgart: Ferdinand Enke, 1975). John Lyons, *Semantics* (Cambridge: Cambridge University Press, 1979), pp. 230–261.

21. Gebser, *Everpresent Origin*, pp. 300–325.

22. Algis Mickunas, "The Dialogical Region," in Joseph Pilotta, ed., *Interpersonal Communication: Essays in Phenomenology and Hermeneutics*, Cen-

ter for Advanced Research in Phenomenology (Washington, D.C.: University Press of America, 1982), pp. 55–68.

23. Maurice Merleau-Ponty, *Visible and Invisible*, trans. A. Lingis (Evanston, Ill.: Northwestern University Press, 1968), p. 104.

24. Alphonso Lingis, "Abject Communication," in Pilotta, *Interpersonal Communication*, p. 168.

25. Mickunas, "The Dialogical Region."

14

Technology Transfer: An African Dilemma

Akin M. Makinde

From the time of Francis Bacon, scientists have written about the possibilities of a more prosperous and advanced society. The emphasis of science has been the control and conquest of nature as a means to this end.[1] It is generally known that a close relationship existed between science and technology in the nineteenth century.[2] This relationship affected not only various industries but also changed human thought and social structure.

As an applied science, many questions are raised concerning the uses and abuses of technology. On the one hand, it has been used to improve human well-being: food production, health care, and education. On the other hand, it brought insecurity, alienation, erosion of privacy, exploitation, and, finally, the potential to destroy society. Rather than promote social peace and human improvement, technology marks an era of violence and destruction.[3] Instead of mastering nature, technology is used to control the individual.[4]

Accordingly, it appears that technology is a two-edged sword.[5] It has both positive and negative effects on the individual and social life. In this chapter, the impact of technology on African nations will be examined, especially from the viewpoint of what is called "technology transfer." While this discussion will apply to Africa in general, all references will be restricted to Nigeria, the largest nation on the African continent.

TECHNOLOGY TRANSFER

Recently, there have been numerous discussions concerning technology transfer. They focus on the importation of technologies from industrial into Third World societies. While generally lauded, this transfer raises various questions that have been suggested by

Denis Goulet.[6] First, is modern technology the key to successful development? Second, will technology deliver on its promise to bring progress to Africa? And third, can technology be transferred from one cultural setting to another in ways that are more beneficial than destructive? In this connection, three key terms are crucial, as proposed by Goulet: "technology," "transfer," and "values." To this is added "impact" or "effect."

Technology is defined as the systematic application of collective human rationality to the solution of problems by asserting control over nature and human activities.[7] Yet what does it mean when people from cultures that have made no significant contribution to creating technological innovations want technology transferred from technologically innovative cultures to their own? From the viewpoint of a culture with advanced technology, transfer means an "exchange from advanced to developing countries of the elements of technical know-how which are normally required in setting up and operating new productive facilities and which are normally in short supply or totally absent in developing economies."[8] This definition, by the British economist Charles Cooper, is unsatisfactory because transfer is treated as simply the physical movement of an object from one location to another, and any other sense is purely metaphorical. Accordingly, Cooper's conception cannot be used because technology transfer remains abstract. Following are the reasons why this is the case.

First, the transfer of technology would mean its total disappearance in one place and reappearance in another without any modification. But it does not make sense to talk of the transfer of technology as if it is merely a commodity. Technology includes science, research, and a variety of production operations. In this sense, the physical transfer of technology does not mean technology transfer.

Second, transfer can only mean the purchase of technological products by nations without technology. Yet this is simply business. Thus, technology transfer is merely another term for selling and buying technological products. As suggested above, technology incorporates protracted scientific research, requiring not only an ability to apply science to practical problems but also a vast educational system. These components of technology cannot be transferred like commodities. Thus, it is more correct to speak of the "commercialization" rather than "transfer" of modern technology. As Goulet writes, "To speak of 'transfers' can be misleading because technology is usually bought and sold internationally in a predominantly seller's market. . . . It is more appropriate to speak of 'circulation' of technology. . . ."[9]

Third, the circulation of technology makes sense only insofar as it represents a reciprocal flow of resources from one nation to another, like the dissemination of knowledge. Thus, the flow of technology from America to Japan need not be asymmetrical. The technology that flows from America to Japan may flow back to America, with innovations provided by Japanese scientific research. Both nations have the capacity for mutual enhancement. But this is not the case when technology takes the form of only finished products that are purchased and consumed at the sellers' markets, as is the case with Africa and the Third World. At present, the term "circulation of technology" is appropriate only for the developed countries, such as United States, Russia, Britain, Japan, Western Europe, and Canada. These nations do not merely consume imported technology but also provide innovations through the circulation of scientific knowledge. This is not the case with the nations of the Third World.

TRANSFER OF TECHNOLOGY AND AFRICA

Although the term "technology transfer" is a misnomer with respect to the Third World, it can serve to distinguish between developed and undeveloped nations and the ways they acquire technologies. One has established technology by the use of science, research, education, and capital investment, the other by purchase. If Africans remain satisfied with the latter conception of transfer, then they are sentenced to be permanently dependent on foreign technology. What is needed to counter this disadvantage is a radical change in the educational policies of African nations, specifically with respect to scientific education. Mathematics must be introduced in addition to various other scientific disciplines. Of course, such an educational policy would have to respect the specific needs of the African populations and cultures. Without this respect, the purchase of mere technological commodities will have drastic results.

This is specifically the case when technology is advertised as the sole means for solving human problems.[10] Because of its efficiency, utility, and success in the industrial nations, technology is sought by the Third World nations. But, as one observer noted, the global diffusion of modern technology tends to standardize the "existence rationality" of all societies around the Western notions of efficiency, rationality, and problem solving.[11] To be modern is to be a technological society. The road to modernity passes through technology because it is assumed that "technology almost certainly offers the best hope of improving the quality of life in the developing countries."[12] Is this assessment adequate? Specifically, just because technology exists, does this mean that one should acquire it in order to be up to date? More important is to judge which technologies are appropriate for African needs, both material and cultural.

This is especially significant since technology is usually adopted to improve a society's material conditions. Yet this excludes the questions of values and the improvement of life in general. Development should mean more than material improvements, particularly when such one-sided growth may degrade the human condition, including a loss of respect for human values, persons, and a society's spiritual well-being, which some observers consider to be necessary for survival in the age of technology.[13] Moreover, technology has become a means of exploitation, dehumanization, and political oppression of innocent citizens.[14] When technology is imported without the requisite scientific culture that produced it, the resulting developments are detached from their roots and become weapons in a cultural vacuum.

Bearing in mind the distinction between the needs of a particular culture and the technological luxuries provided by the sellers' market, the question must be asked whether technology is beneficial or detrimental for African nations. This issue will be examined in terms of technology as a bearer and destroyer of values,[15] and the high price of technology for African nations.[16]

Technology is not merely a means, for it embodies certain values that are also transmitted when it is purchased.[17] One of the values is efficiency. By definition, efficiency requires speed and quick results and disregards such "luxuries" as contemplating and living in harmony with nature, which are important practices in African traditions. Another value associated with technology is "material utility." All phenomena, including nature, social institutions, and human beings, are regarded as objects to be used and manipulated. The value of their existence depends upon how they are used. Thus, even human beings are regarded as something to be controlled, used, and exploited for material gains. When such gains are no longer forthcoming, individuals are discarded.

In contrast, most traditional societies take for granted that persons must live in harmony with nature and other living beings. Even if destructive actions were necessary for survival, atonement would be offered for any suffering that was caused. This attitude is diametrically opposed to the exploitative and destructive one that underpins technological concepts and functions.[18] As the impact of these values on African societies is examined, it will become clear that technology is being acquired at a very high price.

VALUE CONFLICTS

The traditional social life in Africa was communal. All persons owned land on which they peacefully engaged in subsistence farming. The social organization was designed to care for old and young, allowing, in turn, each member of the society both freedom and responsibilities. Accumulation of personal wealth and power, at the expense of others, was regarded as antisocial. Accordingly, each member of a society enjoyed the wealth of the community. Land and natural resources were regarded as gifts from gods to be enjoyed by all. This is part of Julius Nyerere's view of African traditional values, which he insists must be regained and applied to the new African societies.[19] As he states, "In tribal societies, the individuals or the families within a tribe were 'rich' or 'poor' according to whether the whole tribe was rich or poor. If the tribe prospered all the members of the tribe shared in its prosperity."[20]

Along with the above, the following were well recognized as essentials of African social values: extended family, respect for elders, strong family ties, generosity, community spirit, and brotherliness. Life was deemed sacred and only the gods could take it. Family ties were extremely strong and mutual respect prevailed. Obas and chiefs, as the political leaders of tribes, settled disputes and quarrels amicably and maintained social justice and peace. The ailments associated with the complex technological societies, such as stress, stroke, cancer, and anxiety were rare. Pollution was non-existent, as people lived in harmony with nature.

These traditional values began to change during the era of colonialism. The agrarian and industrial revolutions of Europe were transported to Africa by colonialists. Gradually, land became the property of landholders, while an industrial revolution gave birth to both a capitalist and proletariat class. Thus, the seeds of conflict were planted, and the situation worsened with independence.[21] Many African nations gained independence during the second half of this century, when the effects of technology were becoming obvious. And since 1960, events in Africa show a radical departure from traditional values and an acceptance of those imported with the purchase of technology. Within the past two decades "technological transfer" has led to value conflicts between basic developmental needs and what is technologically available. The criterion of the good life is the possession of foreign commodities and technologies at the expense of food production, education, and health care. While agriculture should be the basis for other forms of production, Africans are shifting toward technology as if it can solve all problems without effort. Hence, resources are invested in the most recent, although unadaptable, technologies instead of encouraging self-sufficiency and the preservation of African values. With a sudden oil boom, Nigeria provides a good example.

The Nigerian oil boom was a product of technology. Also, the oil was exchanged for additional foreign technologies. With the acquisition of technology their wealth increased, thus enticing leaders toward selfishness and corruption. This desire to get rich quick was enhanced by the sellers' offering the most recent comforts and novelties. As long as the oil revenues lasted, Nigerians lavished their foreign exchange on innovations that were completely unrelated to their basic developmental needs. In fact, agriculture, the major source of foreign exchange, was abandoned as the population gravitated to big cities to enjoy the products of technology. Government officials made things worse. In order to acquire sudden wealth overnight, much useless technological equipment was bought at highly inflated prices, with commissions ranging from ten to twenty-five percent usually deposited in foreign accounts. With each contract awarded, a lot of money was transferred abroad, that is, as expatriate fees and commissions payable to Nigerians in foreign accounts. It is well known in Nigeria that most of the technological products purchased by the government were never needed and were meant to rot away in some remote corner of the country. For instance, Nigeria does not need the Aerostat balloon for communication. The University of Ife advised against its purchase. But because some people wanted to make money from its purchase the project went ahead, and subsequently about $300 million was wasted before it was abandoned. Examples of such criminal wastes could be found regularly on the pages of Nigerian newspapers for more than a decade. Observers noticed that Nigeria is one of the few oil-producing countries where more than eighty percent of its population did not know that their country was blessed with this resource. The desire to enjoy foreign technological products has led to a wide gulf between the rich and poor, with contractors of technological products and government officials becoming millionaires overnight. In fact, it is now estimated that a few individuals in Nigeria have more money than the national treasury! But the bulk of this stolen money is usually stacked in foreign bank accounts, most notably in Europe and America.

One serious effect of technology transfer is the jealousy it has created between the government and technocrats, most of whom are intellectuals at universities. Probably because they are afraid to become dependent on their own technocrats, the government has never spent much money on university research. Thus, the universities are usually short of funds, while millions of naira are spent on useless projects that bring government officials handsome windfall profits. For this reason, even consulting contracts are given mostly to foreign experts, at about one hundred times their real value. It appears that the more they depend on foreign technology, the greater the opportunity for kickbacks. The result is that a country that used to be rich with oil is now looking to borrow money. The oil boom has become the oil doom, as many Nigerians are now claiming.

Another noticeable effect of technology on African nations can be seen in the city of Lagos. A city that was once beautiful and peaceful before the advent of technology now regularly experiences uncontrollable traffic congestion and all sorts of crimes that were unimaginable twenty-five years ago. Many of the streets in Lagos are no longer safe at night. Armed robbers seem to be beyond the government's control as public executions do not seem to be a deterrent to crime.

Perhaps the bearer of the most destructive effect on African nations is military technology. It brings a double tragedy. First, it is used for massive killing and, second, it is purchased at high cost. Observers of African political affairs are astounded at the number of coups and counter-coups since the advent of military technology in Africa. The acquisition of military hardware often creates huge national debts that force countries into bankruptcy.

THE POLITICS AND ECONOMICS OF TECHNOLOGY TRANSFER

The relationship between the technologically advanced nations and the less developed countries, especially in Africa, is that of master and servant. Just as scientists use scientific knowledge to dominate nature, so have the industrial powers used science and technology to dominate, or at least determine, the economic and political fate of African nations. The dilemma, of course, is that many African leaders cannot do without the big powers. They rely mainly on the imported technologies for their own political survival. Most Africans struggle to enjoy the good things of life that they themselves cannot produce, and it is the belief in Africa that politics is the shortest avenue to sudden power and wealth. Technology offers the clearest path for the acquisition of both. Of course, this requires sapping the resources of the local populations and environment.

Only a cursory look at the huge national debts and trade deficits of the Third World shows the impact of technology on these poor nations. In spite of their oil wealth, the OPEC countries, of which Nigeria is a member, now owe up to $800 billion, most of it to banks in technologically advanced nations. Nine U.S. banks have lent to "risky" countries in various Third World sums of money amounting to more than 250 percent of their capital reserve.[22] Even Latin American countries owe more than $300 billion, while Argentina is reported to have just begun to repay overdue interest on a $44 billion national debt.[23] Yet the tragedy is that the greater part of these debts, now compounded by high interest rates, is used for nonproductive ventures, such as weaponry and prestigious projects, while a substantial percentage of the wealth generated goes to private individuals, thus leaving the citizens poor.

While the war merchants of the industrial nations have exploited Africa through the commercialization of military and other technologies, the phenomenon known as "dumping" remains one of the most serious effects of technology transfer. Some African nations attempt to manufacture technological products locally, but the component parts have to be purchased abroad. For instance, the Nigerian-made Peugeot, assembled in Kaduna, has its parts shipped from France. Such parts are mostly obsolete in the industrialized nations and thus are dumped in the Third World countries. This dumping of obsolete parts and equipment creates an immense problem with respect to rapidly changing technologies. Such equipment must be replaced by newer ones, or spare parts must be made at an inflated cost. Thus, there emerges an unavoidable dilemma: Either purchase new and more expensive gear or fly in experts with parts to repair the old. In either case, huge sums of money are wasted on foreign technology.

Apart from the economics of dumping, there is also a more fundamental issue: health. One example is the dumping of asbestos, despite its known dangers. It has been shown that persons who are exposed to asbestos have a greater risk of asbestosis.[24] Exposure occurs typically through water and air contamination from factories, construction operations involving the spraying of asbestos, the use of crushed stones for highways and driveways, insulation, cement water pipes, cosmetics, and even hair dryers.[25]

Although the manufacture of asbestos-related products was banned in 1978 in the United States, underdeveloped nations have become a ready market for these banned products. Moreover, growing concern is witnessed over the emerging trend of the asbestos industry to relocate in Third World countries, where capital investment and technology are welcomed often without any concern for health and safety regulations.[26] In Nigeria, asbestos has become recently one of the key materials for building technology. The transfer of the asbestos industry also transfers health dangers to the Third World. This type of detrimental transfer of technologies is not an exception, but a rule.

The blame does not rest with the industrialized nations alone. African leaders are eager participants in this process, without recognizing that even if their nations achieve a level of progress akin to that of industrial countries, the problems created by technology will also increase. Drawn into the promise of progress, the leaders of poor nations are hoping for some utopian future; yet such a future might have to be bought at a high price which includes the possibility of human self-annihilation. After all, world competition is technological, with each country attempting to gain an "edge" over others. These conflicts, moreover, may cost Africans their survival. Perhaps this is the ultimate form of international terrorism, threatening nonparticipating populations with punishment for deeds they did not commit.

CONCLUSION

Apart from the emergence of coups and counter-coups, new-found devices for cheating, stealing, invasion of privacy, dehumanization, abuses of human dignity and even murder, technology transfer has eaten deep into the meager resources of African nations. Consequently, apart from the obstacles to rational development and improving the human condition through technology transfer, the expected technological salvation has turned out to be a "technological nightmare." Technology has spawned acquisitiveness, thus undermining the norms of need satisfaction that have enabled Africans to live and survive without the consumption of luxury goods. After more than two decades of familiarity with imported technology, many African nations have been unable to use technology to their own advantage or evolve, by their own scientific intelligence, an appropriate technology. Social norms governing access to and the use of natural resources, which normally are based on equity and priority of needs, were shattered by selfish leaders.[27] All this has destroyed the African norms and values that foster respect for the person.[28] Community spirit has been replaced by the Spenserian view of "every man for himself," as communal solidarity has been abandoned. Furthermore, kinship, friendship, love, marriage, birth, and death have become commercialized.

By adopting technology uncritically, African nations have embraced, just as uncritically, all of the negative aspects associated with it. This is not to argue that Africans should be culturally alienated from the rest of the developed world. Surely, some African traditional values are not worth preserving. The world is too interdependent to be evaluated in terms of some simple values, since communication has led to the convergence of cultures. Nonetheless, Africans must resist the temptation to allow modern technologies and their attendant values to dominate completely some of their own cherished customs. Thus, the synthesis, or integration, of the good and beneficial aspects of traditional values and technological efficiency is highly desirable.

The African nations that, by their indiscriminate purchase of high technology, cannot separate novelties from basic human needs may carry the burden of exploitation and dumping currently associated with technological transfer. If Africans and the Third World cease to be ready markets for military technology, expensive undertakings under the guise of meeting future needs, and various means that lead to human domination, perhaps they will not only be released from the negative impact of technology, but also aid the industrialized nations in diminishing their production of unneeded gadgets that deplete resources.[29] That is, the absence of lucrative markets for destructive technological products in the Third World and, indeed, in Africa, might very well lead to a fundamental reconsideration and reconstruction of the industrialized world's technologically laden political policies. It is hoped that this will lead to the production of needed technologies that are not only commensurate with the productive capacities of African nations but also are adequate for the mutual enhancement of international trading partners. This would make the world not only a safer place, but also offer the African nations opportunities to explore their own needs, develop their own values, and even make their own mistakes. Although it might seem as if there is a great deal of progress in Africa, in reality such technologically induced growth may, in fact, wreck the future of Africa.

NOTES

1. William Leiss, *The Domination of Nature* (New York: George Braziller, 1972), pp. 13–14.

2. Stephen F. Mason, "Science and History," in Stephen F. Mason, ed., *Scientific Thought* (London: Routledge & Kegan Paul, 1966), p. 490.

3. Carroll W. Pursell, Jr., "History of Technology," in Paul T. Durbin,

ed., *The Culture of Science, Technology, and Medicine* (New York: Free Press, 1984), pp. 70–120.

4. Leiss, *Domination of Nature*, p. 14.

5. Denis Goulet, *The Uncertain Promise: Value Conflicts in Technology Transfer* (New York: IDOC/North America Publisher, 1977), Chapter 1.

6. Ibid., p. 3.

7. Ibid., p. 6.

8. Ibid.

9. Ibid., p. 51.

10. Akin M. Makinde, "The Relevance of Modern Mathematics," *Thought and Practice*, 4, no. 1 (1982): 52–60.

11. David Spengler, *Man and Technics* (New York: Alfred Knopf, 1932), p. 20.

12. Ibid.

13. Langdon Gilkey, "The Religious Dilemma of a Scientific Culture," in David Stewart and Donald Borchert, eds., *Being Human in a Technological Age* (Athens: Ohio University Press, 1979), p. 86.

14. George Orwell, *1984* (New York: New American Library, 1983).

15. Goulet, *Uncertain Promise* p. 17.

16. Ibid., pp. 123–144.

17. Dennis Meredith, "Western Technology Abroad," *Technology Review* 77, no. 5. (March/April 1975): pp. 53–54.

18. Goulet, *Uncertain Promise*, p. 20.

19. Julius Nyerere, *Ujaama: Essays on Socialism* (London and New York: Oxford University Press, 1971).

20. Ibid., p. 9.

21. Ibid., p. 11.

22. Harold Lever, "The Debt Threat," *New York Review of Books* 31 (June 28, 1984): 3.

23. John H. Makin, *The Global Debt Crisis* (New York: Basic Books, 1984), pp. 239–242.

24. Samuel S. Epstein, Lester O. Brown, and Carl Pope, *Hazardous Waste in America* (San Francisco: Sierra Club Book, 1982), pp. 19–20, 232, 284.

25. Samuel S. Epstein, *The Politics of Cancer* (New York: Doubleday, 1979), pp. 89–102.

26. Ibid., p. 100.

27. Goulet, *Uncertain Promise*, p. 23.

28. Richard C. Onwuanibe, "The Human Person and Immortality in Ibo (African) Metaphysics," in Theophilus Okere, ed., *African Philosophy* (New York: University Press of America, 1983), pp. 183–198.

29. Regina Cowan, "West German Arms Transfer to Sub-Saharan Af-

rica: Commercialism versus Foreign Policy," in Bruce E. Arlinghaus, ed., *Arms for Africa* (Lexington, Mass.: Lexington Books, 1983), pp. 153–178. See also Paul Goodman, "Can Technology be Humane? in George A. Watkins, ed., *A New Generation of Environmental Essays*, vol. 1 (New York: MSS Information Corporation, 1973), pp. 152–156.

15

Conclusion: Fundamentals of a Responsible Technology

John W. Murphy, Algis Mickunas, and Joseph J. Pilotta

THE TECHNOLOGICAL WORLDVIEW

Most modern thinkers concur with Martin Heidegger that technology is not merely a set of instruments.[1] According to him, "Technology is a mode of revealing,"[2] a way of "bringing forth" the truth.[3] Technology is not only a part of the world, but above all a way of defining it. This is what makes technology a "worldview," both theoretically and practically. Don Ihde adds that technology mediates culture and outlines a unique style of experiencing reality, which he calls "instrumental realism."[4] In this sense, technology not only shapes perception, but, above all, stipulates the parameters of what can be designated as "real." In turn, this reality constitutes a philosophical justification of technology.

According to Jacques Ellul, what threatens society is not the machine and the current wave of computerization per se, but the dehumanizing worldview advanced by technology.[5] Once again, the machine is not simply an instrument but a mechanism for defining reality. Frederick Pollock argues that this ontological shift in the status of the machine is clearly evident subsequent to the invention of cybernetics.[6] And Ellul adds that automation specifies a mode of knowing he calls "technological perception," as technical activity eliminates every nontechnical one or transforms it into technical activity.[7] Additionally, he contends that by eliminating everything that is human, the technological worldview ceases to be responsive to human needs because they are translated into technological imperatives. Stated differently, human needs are transformed into inanimate functions.

Moreover, by structuring perception and social reality, technology cannot solve the problems it generates simply because the solutions that are offered are equally technological and thus may even compound the original difficulties. Thus, the very worldview that subtends technology must be challenged before the question of responsible technology can be posed. Such a challenge requires that this worldview be understood.

Lewis Mumford suggests that one major component of this worldview is an ideology of control. Control means that all activities are guided by the principles of "reason," as opposed to appeals based on emotion.[8] This requires that reason be extricated from experience so that the human-creative side of life is subdued. Most crucial is the fact that this movement toward rationality has become embedded in a material force: technology. Rationality, thus, becomes instrumental, and therefore anything that is not conceivable in terms of material-technical criteria is excluded from reality. In general, the call for rational control of every facet of human activity requires the reduction of everything that is human to matter that can be shaped by technical means. Thus, Mumford points out that technology materializes existence because the world and humans must be regarded as things that can be manipulated.[9] The result, says Heidegger, is that the environment, as well as persons, is perceived to be merely a resource.[10]

In line with this philosophy of control, the world is conceived as "mechanistic" and described as functioning according to precise mathematical laws. Since these laws are deemed to be "ahistorical" and "universal," their application need not respect socio-historical processes. In turn, nature is "demystified" and stripped of any socio-cultural importance.[11] Once this mechanistic and mathematical composition is deemed the only reasonable approach to nature, the socio-cultural world is treated in a similar manner. In short, the latter is also regarded as mechanistic, quantifiable, and ahistorical. The technological worldview not only represents a closed system of thinking, but one that represses the spiritual and creative process and social interaction. Thus, all policy proposals must be evaluated in accordance with technological feasibility and not social desirability, as society is governed by an "ethic" of technology.[12] These are the results of "technological reason," which comes to serve as the sole source of rational norms and correct order.[13]

Maybe the most damaging feature of this worldview is its treatment of humans. As Ellul suggests, humans must be integrated totally into the material domain of existence, for behavior is legitimate only when it can be explained and controlled technologically. This constitutes the "man-machine" complex.[14] Moreover, persons are deprived of what Viktor Frankl[15] calls their "will to meaning," since this hinders a clear perception of "material reality." However, such a view renders persons passive without using direct material force to assault them. According to thinkers such as Herbert Marcuse[16] and Jurgen Habermas,[17] this domination is possible because "instrumental rationality" becomes synonymous with reason. This suppression of human action is called "discipline" by Michel Foucault,[18] for its prevents persons from offering any critique of the technological worldview. In the final analysis, human nature consists of the characteristics that can be manipulated and produced technologically.

What emerges as a social philosophy is functionalism and, as Mumford suggests, an image of a functional society.[19] Functionalism regards society to be a physical or a mechanical system that adheres to the laws of matter. Each part is defined by and assumes a function in the social system that are necessary to maintain order. This provides society with a status that is "objective-ontological," thus portraying order as a reality *sui generis*. All persons are subsequently believed to be controlled by autonomous social laws that, according to Marcuse, comprise an "affirmative culture." This means that persons are considered rational only when they perform their assigned roles in the social system.[20]

In sum, technological understanding, which construes reason to be instrumental, contains the following as elements in its worldview: Reality is purely material; everything is treated mathematically; a technical ethos determines the legitimacy of all personal actions and social policy; all human qualities are either disregarded or reduced to matter; and society is an objective entity existing *sui generis*. These factors guarantee that "subjectivity" is separated from "objectivity," and "rationality" from "irrationality." Thus, they define what is materially possible and not necessarily what is humanly desirable. For Ellul, this is "technological slavery," as the human origin of technology is suppressed.[21] Therefore, increases in technology will not necessarily solve the human problems resulting from its deployment in society.

RESPONSIBLE TECHNOLOGY: A NEW GROUND

The technological worldview, particularly the idea that reason is instrumental, leads to a conception that such reason is "objective" and distinct from conscious experience. In fact, technological reason is presumed to be "knowledge in itself," instead of "knowledge for us." Thus, instrumental reason is accorded an ontological status that is distinct from subjective experiences and wants. This view of reason is yet another version of the traditional dualisms of "objective-subjective," "rational-irrational," and "valid-invalid." In broader terms, it is assumed that what is real is rational and, in narrower terms, what is real is instrumental and material.

But is this dualism valid? Numerous theorists conclude that the special ontological status accorded instrumental reason is indefensible.[22] Instrumental reason need not be posited as purely objective and universal for, after all, it is but one way of conceptualizing the social world. In fact, this style of reasoning is founded on valuation. After the work of Immanuel Kant, William James, and Edmund Husserl it is extremely difficult to posit a pure objectivity of any sort, including instrumental rationality. Husserl, for example, argues that experience is "intentional," and thus technology is part of the "life world" constituted by human activity. In this world, activities are selected, evaluated, and directed toward the fulfillment of human needs that are more than material. This undercuts dualism and suggests that what was once called "objectivity" is actually a product of human intentionality. Others, including Marcuse,[23] Walter Benjamin,[24] and Habermas,[25] suggest that rationality is not only historical but laden with human interests. This further detracts from pure objectivity.

Following this, it is argued that the social world is not something objective but a conjunction of human intentions, activities, and experiences that interpret and select what is relevant, including what is to be done, made, or destroyed. Thus, human experience is "valuative" and selective. The world, says William James,[26] is "acquired perception." Husser[27] calls this the "life world" of intersubjective relations, customs, values, decisions, and activities. As Jean-Paul Sartre[28] argues, the social world consists of "projects" that, while limited by acquired perceptions, also interpret and structure human action. Instrumental reason, thus, does not represent objectivity but a way of structuring the environment in terms of human values and desires. Such reason is not absolute but is mediated by human existence. Hence, technology does not acquire its direction from reason conceived to be transcendent to human existence, but rather from human activities that embody the life world.[29]

If technology is a form of instrumental reason that is at the service of human wants, fulfillment, and interaction, then such reason cannot be said to be paramount in understanding the social world. Even if the illusion is generated that instrumental reason and its technological constructs are most appropriate for understanding and interpreting socio-cultural events, this does not mean that technological rationality cannot be rejected by human experience. For example, the dictum that, if it can be technologically accomplished it must be done, can be tempered by human experience. Consequently, this mediating experience of the life world offers a ground for responsible technology.

LIFE WORLD: CONTEXT FOR RESPONSIBLE TECHNOLOGY

Recently, Edward Ballard raised a provocative question concerning technological development: "Man or technology: Which is to rule?"[30] His reply is that technology can be controlled only by knowledge, which possesses human integrity. Such knowledge is capable of providing goals that delimit the use of technology. Although there is a temptation to claim that science, because it is objective, provides the most appropriate knowledge for determining the social goals to be achieved, scientific information is based on noninstrumental values. Thus, positive science is not necessarily "value free." This is the case for two fundamental reasons: First, science interprets events in accordance with its selected, that is, valued, precepts. Second, science establishes ends and selects means for their achievement. Nowadays, both ends and means are selected to expand technological power. This is precisely the point: The proliferation and growth of technological power is what is valued. Thus, "value freedom" simply obfuscates the values promulgated by the technological worldview. Since this worldview embodies material power, this value is elevated above others and touted to be universally valid knowledge. While claiming to be unbiased, science actively selects a course of action. It pretends to provide "factual knowledge," while actually making such facts and producing the conditions necessary for their verification. For example, technological planning produces facts that are offered as proof that the knowledge that this mode of planning adopts is value free and purely factual. Hence, planning becomes a process that feeds upon itself, while excluding all other views as "opinion."

If technology is value laden in principle, then it must be regarded as mediated by the content of the life world and all that it contains: diverse values, individual and group interests, psychological attitudes, aesthetic concerns, and even religious desires.[31] Therefore, these factors are no less rational than technological values and constructs. All of them are equally factual as components of the social and experienced world. In this sense, technological values and instrumental rationality are but two factors among an entire range of knowledge claims and thus must be balanced against these other considerations. For instance, when planning a nuclear power plant, nontechnical factors should not automatically be dismissed as "emotion," for they may have social value. Simply put, the "stock of knowledge" that regulates a community should be implicated in all technological planning because those reality assumptions are as valid as the ones present in the technological worldview.

Ellul points out that technology is purported to be a servant of the public.[32] Yet if the public is conceived purely in terms of "technological reality," then it is seen abstractly, that is, without an adequate relationship to the life world and its diverse conceptions of reality. To orient oneself to a technocratically conceived audience is to substitute one socio-historically developed reality for an entire socio-cultural community, for technology establishes its own needs as the most legitimate in all domains of social life. This results in a distinction between an "ideal" image of existence and the various values, realities, and desires present in a community.[33] This ideal is deemed to be "reality in itself" and exists apart from human social relationships and activities. As Mumford points out, society becomes an "independent environment."[34] Social order has its own purpose, while its parts are subordinate to the whole, or the ideal.

When a community begins to think that the socio-cultural world is self-generating, its members may begin to adhere to alien forms of life. If a community is told constantly by objective theorists that the values possessed by its members are subjective and hence socially irrelevant, those objective managers may begin to impose their values by selecting particular aims for society: the technological aims valued by these managers. Hence, all other values and concerns become redundant, although they are a vital part of the social fabric. Given these nontechnical concerns and values, technological planning may actually begin to counteract the goals of the citizenry. Nonetheless, the "public" cannot be reduced to or identified with the values of an instrumental reason because a community represents a multiplicity of values, conceptions of reality, interests, and concerns, as opposed to one "true reality."

When the public is equated with various communities that have diverse experiences, people can become self-directing, as they are no longer regarded as subordinate to a reality *sui generis*. Various current writers have suggested how this is to be understood. Foucault[35] regards social self-direction to result from "discourse," while Husserl[36] and George H. Mead[37] refer to this as "intersubjectivity" and "joint action," respectively. This suggests that, since human action mediates knowledge and is implicated in a web of lived interrelationships, then social order must be erected on this activity. As Max Weber notes, order results when persons can anticipate correctly the action of others and not because various so-called objective conditions are present that control behavior. Order grows out of dialogue and intersubjectively understood beliefs and not norms external to the human world. This shift provides the human actor with a central role in the social order.

While such a conception of order does not prescribe how technology shall be used, it does prevent an ethereal rendition of the public from claiming to represent reason and thereby dictating social policy. Multifaceted human interaction promotes a condition that Habermas calls "non-repressive dialogue," which enables an interpersonally negotiated reality and future to be established.[38] When the normative structures of a society are based on this type of human interaction, order is characterized as a contract that contains social contingencies and not absolute, or "scientific," imperatives. Contractual relationships allow a community to hold the future in its hands and to select the means necessary to realize these aims. Even technology must be included within the network of negotiated relationships that form a society. This means that the imperative of technology is given the same validity as other concerns. When society is regarded as dialogical, intersubjectively related, and engaged in negotiating values and truths, the public fulfills its interests and not abstract imperatives.

SOCIAL SENSITIVITY AND TECHNOLOGICAL PLANNING

Whenever a social policy is formulated it should be substantiated by needs assessment. Data must be gathered about a community's desires, interests, and aims so that an appropriate course of action is offered. This process is more complex than it seems, as an appropriate methodology must be designed to collect data. Socially sensitive data can be produced only by a community-based methodology, one that treats social members as intersubjectively related and not a quantified aggregate. It must be stressed that valid knowledge will not be forthcoming automatically merely as a result of technical and logistic refinements made to a methodology. On the contrary, such refinements might even separate further the researcher from the setting under study, thus rendering a needs assessment increasingly insensitive. A community-based methodology does not attempt to deanimate the research process under the pretense of discovering objective or ahistorical "truths." Instead, it must be recognized that human experience inundates the social world and all research activities and that any attempts to deny this will result in the generation of invalid data. A community-based researcher understands the experiences of a community's members and the researcher to be central to social facts and the research process.

In order to grasp the difference between the objective method and a community-based approach, a distinction must be made between facts and meanings. Persons live in a cultural and not an obtrusively material world. As Herbert Blumer[39] argued, community-based researchers are guided by the idea that persons do not respond to objects but to their meaning. And it is this meaning that motivates human behavior. This implies that social action is coextensive with meaning, or human significance, and that this dimension of experience must be appreciated if a community's knowledge base is to be discovered.[40] Furthermore, only when the various levels of meaning present in a community are known can responsible policy formation take place.

In human experience, meaning "makes sense" of events by providing them with an interpretation. Thus, even the material-technological process both is a way of interpreting events and is interpreted in terms of a cultural context. Hence, it might be asked: What does technology mean? Where will it lead? Does it make sense socially? In view of these questions, what begins to appear is a horizon of meaningful social options that serves as the backdrop for making choices about using technology. What a researcher must keep in mind is that the community being "researched" consists of interconnected meanings that provide it with an identity and history. Yet if it is assumed that technological reason is the sole arbiter of rationality, then a community's future will be assessed in technical and, thus, abstract terms.

The key principle of community-based research is what Niklas Luhmann calls "reflexivity."[41] Applied to research, this notion means that the interpretive assumptions made by an investigator, either conceptual or procedural, must be overcome and not simply denied. When researchers recognize reflexively their personal and methodological reality assumptions, it becomes possible to imagine that social life might have a sundry of unique meanings for the members of a community. Simply put, this means that social actions may be interpreted differently in various societies. Similarly, technology may have culturally specific meanings. If people make decisions on the basis of meaning, or what makes sense to them, then they are central to any assessment of a community's needs.

Human experience must guide policy research, for it is this dimension that prescribes the future of a community. Socially sensitive research does not attempt to dominate the world or capture pristine truth, but to interpret a setting in a manner similar to its inhabitants. In order to achieve insight into a setting, a shift must be made away from standardization to reflexivity as a prominent component in the methodology of policy studies. Lacking this component, the experience that supplies social life with meaning will be overlooked. This region of meaning must be explored if a speculative picture of a community's needs and desires is not to supplant those that sustain a community's self-understanding. Community-based research assists a community to identify its own needs and therefore should be called "enablement" research.

COMMUNICATION FOR A RESPONSIBLE SOCIETY

According to Habermas, the issue of responsible planning exposes the tension between science and practical philosophy.[42] As long as science, and its offspring technology, is differentiated from human action, responsible planning is unlikely. What is required for responsible planning is the "dialogical demystification" of science and technology. This means that a community's members, policy makers, and technocrats must contribute equally to the planning process. Such demystification does not call for face-to-face encounters between every individual of every persuasion. Rather, all knowledge bases must be given credence and integrated at the level of experience so that they might all be consulted. Such a dialogue among various knowledge bases not only promotes equivalence between them, but also illustrates order to be predicated on linguistic competence and not normative behavior.

When viewed as normative behavior, communication can easily turn into a monologue that is sustained either by political, economic, or epistemic power, as shown, for example, by Foucault.[43] Normative communication is based on the principle of cognitive uniformity and justified by rules of speech that are thought to be universally valid. Thus, communication takes place when persons conform to specific rules. Habermas argues that this actually represents "distorted communication."[44] What is distorted about it is that speech acts are deemed legitimate only if they mimic a particular cognitive style that claims to be more legitimate than all others because of its objectivity.

On the other hand, when communication is associated with linguistic competence, this style of monologue is avoided. Considering the modern claim that all phenomena are linguistic, or interpreted, to proclaim that "translinguistic" or "objective" rules of speech exist would be a non sequitur. Nonetheless, when understood linguistically all rules of speech are temporary and emerge from human experience. Thus all rules are incarnated in language and constitute intersubjective and not abstract or objective norms. This suggests that rules of speech are never "final" or ultimate but conventionally provisional and mutable. In turn, social norms, values, and policies are instituted intersubjectively through communication. Objectivity makes sense only when a person's actions are anticipated correctly, as opposed to when an empirical referent is designated to be objective.

This shift toward communicative competence has significant consequences for inaugurating a dialogue between various knowledge bases. First, all norms are established linguistically and have a symbolic meaning. Second, their symbolic status means that they do not reveal the reality but an experience or interpretation of reality. Third, because all norms share this dimension of experience, none are ontologically superior to others. Fourth, norms receive their significance from the linguistic-dialogical flux and not because they are inherently valid. Together, these four points create an epistemological equity among knowledge bases required of dialogue. Because all norms are accessible solely through experience, the absolute status required for one cognitive style to dominate another cannot be acquired by any knowledge base.

In this context, technology becomes identified with a particular knowledge base that has limited validity. While outlining its own style of "communicative competence," technology can be challenged because of its association with a specific way of interpreting events. Thus, technology has a living and not a formal character. Not being differentiated from human intersubjectivity, technology can be interrogated with respect to its value in specific social settings. Thus, technological rationality can take its place along with other forms of reason, thereby eliminating its seignorial ontological status. Technology simply becomes one aspect of an intersubjective dialogue that respects all knowledge bases.

This mutual interfacing calls for what Otto Ullrich refers to as "decentralized politics."[45] According to him, the political process has become intimately enmeshed in technological conceptions and practices. It is not "big government" that initiates "big technology" but rather big technology calls for big government. In order to satisfy public needs, technological undertakings that require massive political involvement are initiated at the national or international levels. Yet precisely such expansive governmental operations obscure a community's needs and make persons feel that they have no control over their future. As governmental operations increase in size they distort local values, projects, and options. Yet, according to Ullrich, such expansiveness accompanies the emergence of technical projects. One example relates to the construction of nuclear power facilities.[46] Once such projects are under way, technocratic logic and the scientific community do the rest because large technological projects create big problems. Who is to solve them? Of course, technology is invoked as a political remedy to protect "national interests." For communities are too small, for example, to solve the problems associated with nuclear waste. The irony is that the solutions are mostly imposed on particular communities where this waste is to be "safely" buried. Indeed, the creation of big technologies calls for the generation of increased sources of energy, thus creating bigger problems and the need for bigger solutions.

Decentering the process is one way of involving communities in the creation and utilization of technology. If government-sponsored technology creates problems, why should communities be called upon to solve them? Even if the case could be made that there are overriding national needs, such a viewpoint could be challenged on the basis of community needs and decisions. Nonetheless, as Ullrich notes, a community base provides a "dispersed mediation" that calls for the adaptation of technology to local needs.[47] In other words, many of the problems associated with technology could be avoided if its development were based originally on community needs. Accordingly, a community's political self-management is coextensive with the local mediation of all technocratic means and discourse. Despite the claim of "practicality," government-sponsored technology is basically speculative. It is speculative because the future of humanity, and specifically communities, is wagered on technology without the consent of the citizenry. And when dealing with something as potentially dangerous as technology, developmental policies must be concrete and not abstract.

POSTSCRIPT

According to Habermas, technology can be used responsibly only in a society that has achieved a sense of "mature autonomy."[48] Such a society embodies the aims and conceptions of the tradition of enlightenment: It is both self-directing and self-critical. The future of such a society emerges from human action and not from a metaphysically posited "social system" or form of "reason." Thus, all systems and styles of reasoning must be understood to emerge from a social ethos consisting of community's needs, valuations, and experiences.

In order for technology to further human interests its ontology, or worldview, must be made relative. Technology must be regarded not only as one among various modes of experiencing, but, above all, it must be accommodated to the human life world. Technological rationality cannot dictate *a priori* what life ought to be and which experiences are valid. In addition, technology has to be located within a nonrepressive social ontology that is cognizant of the need for technological rationality to be related to other modes of human experiencing. This eliminates the assumption that technology is "in charge," or directing human development. For if all human experience is the result of action and engagement with the world, then technology is one among other forms of engagement. Thus, as with all other forms of experience, technology has a human base. Once it is perceived in this way, technology can become socially responsible. At this juncture, technology becomes human and society has achieved a sense of mature autonomy.

NOTES

1. Martin Heidegger, "The Question concerning Technology," in Heidegger, *The Question concerning Technology and Other Essays*, trans. William Lovitt (New York: Harper and Row, 1977), p. 5.
2. Ibid., p. 13.
3. Ibid., p. 11.
4. Don Ihde, *Experimental Phenomenology* (New York: G. P. Putnam's Sons, 1977), pp. 139–143. See also Don Ihde, *Technics and Praxis* (Dordrecht: D. Reidel, 1979), pp. 3–39.

5. Jacques Ellul, *The Technological Society*, trans. John Wilkinson (New York: Random House, 1964), pp. 319–344.

6. Frederick Pollock, *The Economic and Social Consequences of Automation* (Oxford: Basil Blackwell, 1957), p. 83.

7. Ellul, *The Technlogical Society*, p. 83.

8. Michel Foucault, *Discipline and Punish*, trans. Alan Sheridan (New York: Pantheon Books, 1977), pp. 56ff.

9. Lewis Mumford, *Technics and Civilization* (New York: Harcourt, Brace and World, 1963), pp. 31ff.

10. Heidegger, "Question concerning Technology," pp. 18–19.

11. Mumford, *Technics and Civilization*, p. 12.

12. Ellul, *The Technological Society*, p. 134.

13. James M. Curtis, *Culture as Polyphony* (Columbia: University of Missouri Press, 1978), pp. 11–17.

14. Ellul, *The Technological Society*, pp. 395ff.

15. Viktor E. Frankl, *Psychotherapy and Existentialism* (New York: Simon and Schuster, 1967), pp. 5–13.

16. Herbert Marcuse, *One Dimensional Man* (Boston: Beacon Press, 1964), pp. 17–18.

17. Jurgen Habermas, *Theory and Practice*, trans. John Viertel (Boson: Beacon Press, 1974), pp. 268–282.

18. Michel Foucault, *Discipline and Punish* (New York: Pantheon Books, 1977), pp. 73–103.

19. Mumford, *Technics and Civilization*, p. 30.

20. Herbert Marcuse, "The Affirmative Character of Culture," in Marcuse's *Negations* (Boston: Beacon Press, 1969), pp. 88–133.

21. Ellul, *The Technological Society*, p. 84.

22. Hubert L. Dreyfus, *What Computers Can't Do* (New York: Harper and Row, 1979), pp. 1–66.

23. Herbert Marcuse, "On Hedonism," in Marcuse's *Negations* (Boston: Beacon Press, 1969), pp. 159–200.

24. Walter Benjamin, "Theses on the Philosophy of History," in Hannah Arendt, ed., *Illuminations* (New York: Schocken Books, 1969), pp. 253–264.

25. Jurgen Habermas, *Knowledge and Human Interest* (Boston: Beacon Press, 1971), pp. 196ff.

26. William James, *Essays in Radical Empiricism* (Cambridge: Harvard University Press, 1976), pp. 30–36.

27. Edmund Husserl, *The Crisis of European Sciences and Transcendental Phenomenology*, trans. David Carr (Evanston: Northwestern University Press, 1970), p. 113.

28. Jean-Paul Sartre, *Being and Nothingness*, trans. Hazel E. Barnes (New York: Philosophical Library, 1956), pp. 94–105.

29. Husserl, *The Crisis of European Sciences and Transcendental Phenomenology*, pp. 48–55, 142–144.

30. Edward G. Ballard, "Man or Technology: Which Is to Rule?" in Stephen Skousgaard, ed., *Phenomenology and the Understanding of Human Destiny* (Washington, D.C.: University Press of America, 1981), pp. 3–30.

31. Alfred Schutz and Thomas Luckmann, *The Structures of the Life-World* (Evanston, Ill.: Northwestern University Press, 1973), pp. 9–11.

32. Ellul, *The Technological Society*, p. 390.

33. Chaim Perelman, *The New Rhetoric and the Humanities* (Dordrecht: D. Reidel, 1979), pp. 48–50.

34. Mumford, *Technics and Civilization*, p. 324.

35. Michel Foucault, *The Archealogy of Knowledge*, trans. A. M. Sheridan Smith (New York: Harper and Row, 1972), pp. 104–105.

36. Edmund Husserl, *Cartesian Meditations* (The Hague: Nijhoff, 1973), pp. 89–151.

37. George Herbert Mead, *The Philosophy of the Act* (Chicago: University of Chicago Press, 1938), pp. 152–153.

38. Jurgen Habermas, *Theory and Practice*, trans. John Viertel (Boston: Beacon Press, 1973), pp. 19–40.

39. Herbert Blumer, *Symbolic Interactionism: Perspective and Method* (Englewood Cliffs, N.J.: Prentice-Hall, 1969), pp. 132–139.

40. Edward G. Ballard, *Man and Technology* (Pittsburgh: Duquesne University Press, 1978), pp. 87–114.

41. Niklas Luhmann, *Soziologische Aufklaerung*, vol. 1 (Opladen: Westdeutscher Verlag, 1970), pp. 92–112.

42. Habermas, *Theory and Practice*, pp. 1–5.

43. Foucault, *Discipline and Punish*, pp. 138–143.

44. Jurgen Habermas, "Toward a Theory of Communicative Competence," in Hans Peter Dreitzel, ed., *Recent Sociology*, vol. 2 (New York: Macmillan, 1970), pp. 114–148.

45. Otto Ullrich, *Technik und Herrschaft* (Frankfurt am Main: Suhrkamp, 1977), p. 405.

46. Ibid., p. 370.

47. Ibid., pp. 370–375.

48. Habermas, *Theory and Practice*, p. 17.

Selected Bibliography

Angus, Ian H. *Technique and Enlightenment: Limits of Instrumental Reason*. Washington, D.C.: University Press of America, 1984.
Angus's volume offers an examination of technological rationality from a phenomenological perspective.

Ballard, Edward G. *Man and Technology*. Pittsburgh: Duquesne University Press, 1978.
A thorough introduction to the philosophical significance of technology is offered.

Bell, Daniel. *The Coming of the Post-industrial Society*. New York: Basic Books, 1973.
Bell discusses the role of technology in shaping the workplace of the future.

Berger, Peter L.; Brigitte Berger; and Hansfried Kellner. *The Homeless Mind*. New York: Random House, 1973.
The alienating effects of technology in the modern world are examined.

Blum, Henrik. *Planning for Health*. New York: Human Sciences, 1981.
This book deals with the health care "system," while illustrating various approaches to planning.

Braverman, Harry. *Labor and Monopoly Capital*. New York: Monthly Review Press, 1974.
This book reveals how technology has been used as a mechanism of social control at the workplace.

Cooley, Mike. *Architect or Bee? The Human Technology Relationship*. Boston: South End Press, 1980.
Cooley offers an analysis of how technology transforms the workplace.

Dewey, John. *Experience and Education*. New York: Collier Books, 1963.
Dewey develops a technological consciousness of education that is thoughtful, wide ranging, and winsome. A critical reading of this work will help the reader come to grips with the limitations of technological consciousness.

DiFazio, William. *Longshoremen: Community and Resistance on the Brooklyn Waterfront*. South Hadley, Mass.: Bergin and Garvey, 1985.
    The impact technology has had on changing work on the waterfront is assessed.

Dreyfus, Herbert. *What Computers Can't Do*. New York: Harper and Row, 1979.
    An analysis is offered of the cognitive style that accompanies the onset of computerization.

Ellul, Jacques. *The Technological Society*. trans. John Wilkinson. New York: Random House, 1964.
    The rationale that sustains the apparent autonomy of technology is examined. This book remains a classic in the area of technological studies.

Forester, John, ed. *Critical Theory and Public Life*. Cambridge: M.I.T. Press, 1985.
    This collection of essays evaluates the relevance of Jurgen Habermas's thought for social planning.

Foucault, Michel. *The Birth of the Clinic*. trans. A. M. Sheridan Smith. New York: Vintage Books, 1975.
    The history of the rationalization of the practice of medicine is documented.

———. *Discipline and Punish: The Birth of the Prison*. trans. Alan Sheridan. New York: Pantheon Books, 1977.
    The impact of reason on conceptualizing punishment is revealed.

———. *The History of Sexuality, vol. 1: An Introduction*. trans. Robert Hurley. New York: Pantheon Books, 1980.
    In this book, Foucault illustrates how technological rationality transforms the body into an object.

Friedson, Eliot. *Doctoring Together: A Study of Professional Social Control*. New York: Elsevier, 1976).
    The problems that are associated with the professional control of medicine are explored.

Galtung, Johan. *Development, Environment, and Technology: Towards a Technology for Self-Reliance*. New York: United Nations, 1979.
    This study addresses the impact of technology on the quality of the human environment and social growth in developing nations.

Gillett, Margaret. *Educational Technology: Toward Demystification*. Scarborough, Ontario: Prentice-Hall, 1973.
    Gillett discusses the charge that technology dehumanizes the education process.

Gorz, Andre. *Farewell to the Working Class*. Boston: South End Press, 1982.
    The effects of industrialization on the labor force are discussed.

Habermas, Jurgen. *Legitimation Crisis*. trans. Thomas McCarthy. Boston:

Beacon Press, 1975.

Habermas analyzes the role technological rationality plays in integrating modern capitalist societies.

———. *Toward a Rational Society*. trans. Jeremy J. Shapiro. Boston: Beacon Press, 1970.

These essays discuss the political role of experts, the relationship of technology to the polity, and the function technological rationality plays in legitimizing modern society.

Heidegger, Martin. *The Question concerning Technology and Other Essays*. trans. William Lovitt. New York: Harper and Row, 1977.

This collection contains Heidegger's classic essay on technology, in which he explores the worldview outlined by technolgical rationality.

Ihde, Don. *Technics and Praxis*. Dordrecht: D. Reidel, 1979.

Idhe has compiled a collection of his articles that deal with the philosophy of technology.

Illich, Ivan. *Medical Nemesis: The Expropriation of Health*. New York: Bantam Books, 1977.

Illich's thesis is that technology makes patients and doctors dependent on technical rationality, while making them insensitive to their own bodies, environment, and social needs.

Luhmann, Niklas. *The Differentiation of Society*. trans. Stephen Holmes and Charles Larmore. New York: Columbia University Press, 1982.

The essays in this volume address a wide range of topics, including the temporal and structural character of modern society.

Marcuse, Herbert. *One-Dimensional Man*. Boston: Beacon Press, 1964.

This is Marcuse's classic statement on technology as a mode of social control.

Mumford, Lewis. *Technics and Civilization*. New York: Harcourt, Brace and World, 1963.

The characteristics of the technological worldview are outlined.

O'Neill, John. *Five Bodies: Studies in Radical Anthropomorphism*. Ithaca, N.Y.: Cornell University Press, 1985.

The writings of contemporary European philosophers are applied to studying the body.

Perrucci, R. *Circle of Madness: On Being Insane and Institutionalized in America*. Englewood Cliffs, N.J.: Prentice-Hall, 1974.

This is an observational study of life in a mental hospital, which offers valuable insight into what it is like to be a patient in this type of institution.

Pilotta, Joseph J., ed. *Interpersonal Communication: Essays in Phenomenology and Hermeneutics*. Washington, D.C.: University Press of America, 1982.

This collection of essays examines key theoretical and methodological issues that are related to communication research.

Pollock, Frederick. *The Economic and Social Consequences of Automation.* Oxford: Basil Blackwell, 1975.

A classic statement is offered on the philosophy that provides technology with the illusion of autonomy.

Reiser, Stanley. *Medicine and the Reign of Technology.* New York: Cambridge University Press, 1978.

This is a key source for documenting the historical development of medical technology.

Rifkin, Jeremy. *Algery: A New World.* New York: Penguin Books, 1983.

This book provides a basic orientation to the political implications of biotechnology.

Rosen, G. *Madness in Society: Chapters in the Historical Sociology of Mental Illness.* Chicago: University of Chicago Press, 1968.

Rosen provides a well-documented history of mental illness.

Sabato, Larry J. *The Rise of Political Consultants.* New York: Basic Books, 1983.

The technological selling of a political campaign is assessed.

Schell, Jonathan. *The Fate of the Earth.* New York: Avon Books, 1982.

Schell's work chronicles the embodied history of mankind, or its existential character.

About the Contributors

DELYSA BURNIER is professor of political science at Ohio University, Athens.

KAREN A. CALLAGHAN is Director of Program Evaluation, Consolidated Youth Services, Jonesboro, Arkansas.

LISA A. CALLAHAN is Director of Criminology Research, State University of New York, Albany.

DAVID DESCUTNER is professor of communication at Ohio University, Athens.

WILLIAM DIFAZIO is associate professor of sociology at St. John's University, New York City.

JOHN FORESTER is professor of urban studies at Cornell University, Ithaca, New York.

JOSEPH F. FREEMAN is professor of political science at Lynchburg College, Lynchburg, Virginia.

DENNIS R. LONGMIRE is assistant dean of the School of Criminal Justice at Sam Houston State University, Huntsville, Texas.

AKIN M. MAKINDE is professor of philosophy at the University of Ife, Ile-Ife, Nigeria.

ESTHER S. MERVES is assistant professor of sociology at Kenyon College, Gambier, Ohio.

LARRY A. NUTTBROCK is assistant professor of sociology at Arkansas State University, Jonesboro.

JOHN O'NEILL is professor of sociology at York University, Toronto.

JOHN R. SCUDDER, JR., is professor of philosophy at Lynch-burg College, Lynchburg, Virginia.

TIM L. WIDMAN is a doctoral candidate in the communication department at Ohio State University, Columbus.

Index